It's All About Attitude

loving and
living well
with autism

Kathy Almeida

Gayle Nobel

It's All About Attitude

loving and

living well

with autism

DESERT
Beach
PUBLICATIONS

For information, contact
Desert Beach Publications
P.O. Box 14
Belleview, FL 34421
www.desertbeachpublications.com

Editor: Andrea Beaulieu, Andrea Beaulieu Creates
Cover and Text Design: Bill Greaves, Concept West
Production Editor: Michele DeFilippo, 1106 Design
Photo (Nobel family): Cheswick Photography

Library of Congress Control Number: 2006901130
ISBN-13: 978-0-9777284-0-4
ISBN-10: 0-9777284-0-4

To Mark and Kyle

Acknowledgements

To our families, friends, and the people we met only for a moment, thank you for being our "believing mirrors" on this journey. We love and appreciate all of you!

For your support by reading our rough drafts and giving us great feedback: Kim Isaac, Kara Hume, Christy Maxey, Robin Asaki, Pauline Banducci, Paula and Harvey Begay, Judy Kendall, Jerry Florman, Neil Nobel, Daryl Lanier, Paul Jacobs, Jo Kittinger, and Laura Allen.

A big thanks to Michael for listening to us read most of our book at Crescent Beach, and to Daryl for also listening to us read and reread our work on St. Pete beach. Kim, thanks for your endless encouragement, support, and enthusiasm, as well as your special love for Kyle.

To Sylvia Nobel, thanks for being so kind to us and helpful in offering support, words of wisdom and information. To Hada Almeida, for always believing in her daughter-in-law's gifts as an artist. To Dr. Talmor, thank you for always being there for us.

With appreciation to Sarah Swindell, a new traveler on this journey, for her inspiration and encouragement. To Carrie Bell, thanks for listening and offering support from one who has "been there," and Moe Bell, for the wisdom of your experience. Thank you, Terry Grant, for being there to hold my hand in the very beginning.

To our creative team who helped us put our book together:

A big thanks to our editor, Andrea Beaulieu, who, with lots of patience and understanding for her new fledglings in the writing world, helped us hone our writing skills and clarify our thoughts and words.

With gratitude to our graphic designer, Bill Greaves, who designed our book.

Thanks to Michele DeFilippo, our typesetter, who educated us on format.

From Kathy:

To my parents, Paul and Roberta, thank you for the gift of my life and always your love, without which I would not be the person I am. And to Paul, my brother and Daryl, my sister and your families—thank you for being here for me. I love each of you!

To Chrissi, Eric and Noah. For being part of our lives. I love you!

To Michael, my rock, thank you for being you. Your love for your brother inspires and touches me daily, showing me what a special human being you are. I love you!

To Frank, my husband, friend, and partner, thank you for believing in and supporting me, and for sharing life with me. But most of all, for being the person you are, and for loving our sons and me. I love you!

To Gayle, my friend and coauthor: In a world where most people couldn't understand, it has been the greatest gift for me to know you were there and did "get it." I am so happy to have shared our journey together as moms, and now as friends making this dream real. Thank you for being you!

From Gayle:

To my parents, Alex and Marilyn, who are no longer with us, thanks for your love and encouragement.

To Judy, my "other" mom, thanks for your love, support, and wisdom.

Philip, thanks for waiting on me. It's been nice reconnecting with you.

With love and appreciation to my wonderful daughters Rachel and Leah, thanks for cheering me on throughout the process of writing this book. You both share the limelight next to your brother with grace and humor. Our "girl times" refresh and recharge my soul.

To Neil, my wonderful husband, who supported me throughout the entire process, frequently offering words of encouragement, inspiration, and love, and who smiled and cooked breakfast throughout all the years of Saturday morning phone calls. Thanks for being a great father.

A very special thank you to my friend and coauthor, Kathy, who first encouraged me to find my writing voice and inspired me to keep going. I never would have done this without you. Thanks for being there. Your friendship has been a true blessing in my life.

~ ~ ~

To Mark and Kyle: You are the heart and soul behind the making of this book, for without you, there would be no book. Thank you, first and foremost, for being the people you are and for the gifts you have so patiently tried to give us. We are forever grateful. But, most of all, we are honored to be able to know and love each of you.

To God: It all begins and ends with You. Keep working on us, we'll get there yet!

Contents

Foreword

You have picked up this book for a reason. Maybe your child has been diagnosed with autism. Perhaps you know someone whose child has autism or some other affliction.

You know your life has changed. The responsibilities for caring for such a child, or adult, does not easily balance with the demands of your job, duties to your other children, or attention to your spouse. Where will you find room for yourself? Where and how will you find the strength?

These are not easy questions to answer. But two remarkable women have shown me it can be done. And it can be done with a life spirit that is both uplifting and inspiring to all who have known them. They have persevered in certainly one of life's biggest challenges with love left over for all and, yes, even energy for their own personal fulfillment. How do they do it? Why do they do it?

This book is not a "how to" book. It is not a book on new interventions for autism or the latest teaching methods. This is a "why to" book—a book that will inspire and assist you in all that is ahead.

Frankly, you don't know exactly what will work for your child. Due to his or her uniqueness, changing medical developments, and the age-related changes that naturally occur, you will not be in a position to get any permanent answers. But you can know what you want for them, what you want for your family, and what you want out of your life. This will be the only constant in a sea of change. Without such a rudder, you will feel adrift, vulnerable to the next wave, or the next set of opinions. It need not be that way.

This book is for you. Your inner peace and your strength are what will get you through. Without these, you might not do the best you could for your special child, and you might not have the residual energy for the rest of your family responsibilities. Will this be a journey of love and acceptance, or a grim slog where you constantly resent the cosmic forces that put you in this spot?

The choice is yours. This book will help you throughout your journey. Listen to the words of two women who have learned how to do extraordinary things.

—*Neil Nobel*

Introduction

It is our hope that what we share in this book will touch your hearts and spirits, providing emotional soul food as well as compassion and camaraderie. May our words offer you inspiration for the journey with your special child. We invite you to create a vision filled with endless possibilities for both you and your child. Here are our stories.

In the Beginning

What can a stay-at-home mom and writer possibly tell you about autism? Plenty. I have experienced twenty-one years with my son, who has autism. I may not have gone to all the schools and earned the special education requirements to teach "Autism 101," but I can tell you the ins and outs from seeing it first hand. As a parent, I believe I have something to offer other parents trying to find their own way to love and help their cherished ones who have special needs or circumstances.

My own story begins when Mark was born. At his first cry, I wanted to protect and help him, sensing something different and special. From that day until today, I've learned how to do just that. It has been an amazing journey, taking each of us—me, my husband Frank, and Michael (our first-born son and Mark's brother)—around many winding roads. We traveled up some very steep grades to get where we are now—not to the top of the hill, or to the end of our journey, but to a place where we are skilled travelers, much better adapted to our path than when we first began.

Mark was born in a normal delivery, but from the minute he got home, he spent most of his days crying. I breastfed him, but everything I ate seemed to upset his delicate and sensitive system. When he wasn't crying, he was a sweet, happy, and loving baby, very alert to his world. At around nine months, he walked and talked. At twelve months, he started having seizures—not often, just one or two a month. By eighteen months, he was withdrawn, shared no eye contact, and had stopped talking.

We began going to doctors at the first sign of seizures. Mark was diagnosed with epilepsy and started taking all sorts of drugs. As he learned to live on the different medications—some made him quite sick—we kept searching for ways to help him. When the standard treatments didn't seem to work, we explored different diets and alternative treatments. We became vegetarians so we could provide as healthy a diet as possible for our son. We also tried speech therapy, and other special schools that turned out to be invasive and less than respectful to the children they were trying to help.

During this time, we became aware Mark also had autism. We'd seen an article listing the ten signs of autism, and Mark had all ten. I also came across an article by Barry Neil Kaufman in *Mothering Magazine* recounting how he and his wife were able to help their son recover from autism by creating a unique, home-based program. When I read the article, I felt as if I'd come home. In the article, I read the answer I'd been looking for—what to do next to help Mark.

After discussing the article with my husband, we both decided to give the Option Institute a try. In September 1984, Frank, Mark, and I, flew to Massachusetts and spent an amazing week at the Option Institute. We learned how to set up our own home-based program. We also discovered one of the best ways to help Mark was to change ourselves—to become more accepting and loving of him. By doing this, we were able to become his best teachers, advocates, and guides.

Once home we started our own home-based program, training friends and family to help as volunteers. They worked with Mark and gave us much-needed breaks. We ran the program seven days a week, from the moment he woke up until the moment he went to bed, for more than ten years. It was quite an undertaking, but one that enriched us all. Everyone was touched by Mark's unique and special soul. Under each person's love and care, he was able to grow and make sense of a world that made no sense to him at all when we first began.

Two years after starting the program, Frank and I went to the Parent Intensive Week at the Option Institute to continue learning and to be with other parents doing similar programs. This is where we met Gayle. I remember the first time I saw her. We were sitting in a circle in one of our classroom sessions and I looked at the person across the room from me. She smiled. Later, at break, we talked and felt an instant connection. Frank was drawn to her too and thought she and I looked alike. That was the beginning of our long and wonderful friendship.

After Mark's home-based program ended, he and I fell into a routine of spending our days together. We worked on school subjects and took lots of long walks. Our favorite place to walk was to a neighboring farm just up the road. We were welcome anytime. We walked around the land and enjoyed watching their herd of cows. The farm was such a beautiful and peaceful place.

One day, Frank came home from work and said he wanted to show me a piece of property he was interested in buying for us. It turned out to be the farm Mark and I visited each day.

We bought fifty acres of the farm and built a huge barn on it. We spent hours there, enjoying our new land. Mark and I walked there every day. Three years ago, we built a new home on the property, where the four of us now live with our dog and three cats. We share the land with our seven cows and a bull. Birds, rabbits, turtles, fox squirrels, and foxes like to visit as well.

Mark loves our new home, where he roams and explores the land. He enjoys having family and friends over for holidays, dinners, and just to visit. He and I still enjoy taking lots of walks and going to the beach. One of his favorite things to do is to go to the Gator Basketball games in Gainesville with Frank and Michael. He's a huge fan.

Mark continues to grow and learn. He teaches us things like acceptance, compassion, courage, strength, laughter, joy, the belief that anything is possible, and most importantly, love, just by being the person he is.

As you look into the windows of our lives, I hope you will be inspired by our gifts of attitude and love, just as we have been.

Kathy Almeida

In December 1983, my husband Neil and I became the proud parents of our first child, Kyle. We had been married for three and a half years, and after teaching children with learning disabilities in the public schools, I was ready to stay home with my new baby boy. When it became evident Kyle had special needs, I embarked on a mission to learn as much as possible about how to help him and us.

Just before Kyle's third birthday, in the midst of one of his most difficult, out-of-control seizure periods, our daughter, Rachel, was born. We were in awe at the ease with which she developed, especially in contrast to Kyle's constant struggles. Many times I nursed Rachel, vigilantly watching for Kyle's next seizure. While my heart ached for Kyle, it overflowed with gratitude and joy for Rachel.

In my search for ways to help Kyle, I remembered reading the book, *Son Rise,* in college. Both Neil and I were immediately attracted to this very respectful and unique way of working with an autistic child. We were thrilled to discover we could receive training in the Son Rise program. So, in April 1988, with eighteen-month-old Rachel and grandpa in tow, Neil and I took Kyle, then four, to Massachusetts to learn how to create a Son Rise-style program in our home. We learned techniques designed to help reach and teach Kyle. More importantly, we were introduced to the attitude, the most significant feature of the program. I would hold on to this "attitude anchor" throughout the many challenges we encountered as Kyle grew.

This attitude, along with Neil's wonderful support, was my key to moving beyond initial despair to a better acceptance of autism. We learned our attitude could make or break our day, our teaching session, our lives, and even a single moment with Kyle. As the heartache began to subside, I discovered I could feel joy and gratitude for Kyle, too.

We returned home to round up and train volunteers to help us work with Kyle. Unknown to me at the time, on the other side of the country, Kathy and Frank were preparing to start a similar journey with their son, Mark.

Less than a year after beginning our home program, we welcomed our beautiful daughter Leah into the world. I took on the challenge of trying to balance the needs of the girls with the demands of running a home program for Kyle. My days were filled with sessions in Kyle's play-room, staff observations and training, and time spent with Rachel and Leah. I assumed the role of typical mom with my daughters, taking them to parks, restaurants, friend's homes, and dance classes. With my son, I took on the additional role of teacher, program manager, and advocate. It was quite a juggling act.

In the early years, because of his intense program schedule, most of our activity with Kyle was separated from our time with the girls. I regret this separation, as it set a family dynamic in motion that continued throughout the rest of their childhood and teen years.

In February 1991, I attended an advanced training program for fam-ilies doing the Son Rise program. There, I met Kathy and Frank Almeida. Little did I know Kathy and I would become close friends in the years to come, supporting each other via long distance phone con-versations, and later on, by email. Our friendship blossomed as we shared our experiences, laughing and supporting each other through the challenging times.

In 2001, with Kyle starting high school full time, and Rachel and Leah busy being teenagers, I had more time and was ready for a new endeavor. So, it was during one of our famous Saturday morning phone calls, Kathy and I decided to write a book together. Over the previous few years, Kathy had successfully prodded me to join her by dabbling with writing. A book seemed like a natural next endeavor. Without really knowing where the idea would take us, we each began putting our hearts on the page as we lived daily with our families and autism.

Our dream to make a difference for others on similar paths quickly evolved into an incredible vehicle for personal awareness and growth. The writing process also became a wonderful extension of our friendship, adding a new dimension to our relationship and giving us yet another excuse to get together. With each essay, we created a snapshot of the journey we have traveled separately, and yet parallel to one another.

As Kathy encouraged my writing from the East Coast, my family cheered me here at home. They truly are a blessing. In the midst of my life's chaos, I am enveloped by the love and support of Neil, Kyle, Rachel and Leah Nobel. Each is an incredible gift to me, and for this, I am eternally grateful.

Gayle Nobel

Kyle

Birthdays

Gayle

Preparing to celebrate Kyle's eighteenth birthday, I reflect.
My first child, a perfect baby boy.
Excitement and uncertainty,
Breastfeeding and bonding,
Loving and cuddling,
Interrupted sleep, his first smile.
Fear and despair, his first seizures, his first time in the hospital,
Unanswered questions,
Not knowing.
A diagnosis,
Epilepsy.

Medication and side effects,
Adjusting expectations and then waiting.
What does it all mean?
Watching and noticing things aren't right.
He's not like others his age; something is missing.

Milestones gained and then sometimes lost,
First steps so slowly taken, with us as guides and cheerleaders.
First words so sweet; relief.

More seizures and medication,
The words disappear, never to return.

A diagnosis,
Autism.
I was right, something was so very different about my boy.
More birthdays, and gradually, I learn to look outside the box and see
*   differently.*
I cry, but I laugh too,
Bittersweet love for my mysterious boy.

Many years spent trying to reach our son in a home program,
Love and acceptance as our guides, attitude is key.
Sometimes we reach him and many days we don't;
We persevere.
Years go by and a gentle soul is created.
I don't notice how much I am growing at the same time.
I keep asking: Could I be happy if he never changes? Would it be okay if
*   we never fix him? Will I ever stop feeling the angst, the struggle?*

I learn to celebrate the tiny steps,
Finding ways to connect, we continue to do the impossible.

Kyle attends weddings, movies, and school,
Rides horses, shops and climbs mountains,
He grows and learns more in his teen years than ever before;
A home gym, not a car, for his eighteenth birthday.

When did I stop wanting to fix him?
When did I realize that I am happy even if he never changes?
When did I give up the struggle and stop mourning for the son
*   I didn't get?*

When did I get so high up on the mountain called acceptance that
*   I laughed more than I cried?*
Must have been all those birthdays.

The gift of time,
Seeing differently and appreciating the small steps, redefining miracle,
All key lessons on my journey
In learning to live well with autism,

It's all about attitude.

*"The thread of our friendship is woven through
and around our stories."*

A Gift of Grace

Friendship

Kathy

Today is Valentine's Day, the day of love. It is also the birthday of my friend and coauthor, Gayle. I am glad we met and became friends. I imagine our paths would have turned out very differently without our friendship to guide, support, protect, encourage, and sustain us as we traveled this special journey.

Before Mark was born, I knew nothing about seizures or autism. Today, it's a different story; I've become quite familiar with both. It has been amazing and wonderful to share my experiences with someone who can completely relate to my circumstances. We've helped each other to grow, and to see things more clearly when we weren't able to do so by ourselves. We've encouraged each other to take steps we were afraid to take. We've listened to each other's stories about our other loves, but have always come back to the special love for our sons that brought us together.

In our journey together, we have grown as individual women, discovering our own strengths—some we weren't even aware we had—and finding our own distinct way as we traveled this path together, yet separately. While we live on opposite sides of the country, that hasn't stopped or hurt our friendship. It's probably been a good thing. If we lived closer to each other, we'd probably spend all our days talking on the phone or at each other's homes. This way, the need to keep an eye on our pocketbooks frees us to actually live our lives instead of just talking about them.

Gayle inspires me with her dedication and love for Kyle. Sometimes I think her road is much harder than my own, and that the universe senses that and provides for her by sending excellent help for her son.

I also feel lucky to have her to talk with—to be my confidant. So often when we talk, our conversations turn out to be incredibly creative. We start out in one place, seeing things one way, and by the time we've finished, we have traveled to a totally new and better place, often with solutions and suggestions that weren't there for us when the conversation started. I love those times. They are stimulating, refreshing, and definitely God-inspired. I know that God is watching, protecting, and talking to each of us through the other.

Now we've taken a new step in our friendship, putting down on paper some of what we've learned, and are learning, on this quest. We are challenging each other to grow again so we can be there for others, as well as for each other. Hopefully, the lessons we've learned will make the path easier for those who follow, like helping hands pointing the way on that steep mountain trail when it turns tricky and feels scary.

We are blessed to have each other, because often we have no idea where we're going, much less how we're going to get there. We've learned to laugh and not take our journeys, or ourselves, so seriously. Inspired by God, we are walking in uncharted land and, like Lewis and Clark, creating our own maps. Only this time, it's us, two friends, walking with our very special sons.

Serendipity

Gayle

I met Sarah in the bookstore by sheer coincidence. I was in line, waiting for help, and heard her ask the clerk for help locating books on autism. She was obviously still raw from her son's brand new diagnosis because when I told her that I, too, had a son with autism, the tears came easily.

I immediately had a strong desire to give her something, and I knew it had to be more than the latest intervention to try or book to buy. What could I offer, in that moment, knowing I might never have contact with her again? I wanted to sum up eighteen years of experience and share some profound words of wisdom. So, with a sense of urgency, I fumbled for words: "Though I know it doesn't seem like it right now, your little boy is an amazing gift to you. Not the one you expected, but one that will change your life and transform you in remarkable ways." Now we were both teary eyed.

As it turned out, this serendipitous meeting with Sarah transformed me as well. By reflecting on Sarah's questions, I was able to gather together what I had learned—the things that had made a difference for me over the years—and record them. In the week that followed, I wrote Sarah a long letter, a mini-guidebook of sorts. Kathy and I had just begun writing this book, so in many ways, this letter became my outline and writing guide.

In the months that followed, Sarah and I became friends. Through supporting Sarah, I lifted myself up as well. In answering her questions, I became inspired to live those answers. As I shared with Sarah, I taught myself, once again, the keys to feeling good, living well, and making a difference for Kyle. I became stronger and more confident as I relearned my own lessons.

One of the many pivotal questions Sarah asked was, "What would you do differently if you had it to do over?" As I explored this, I realized how amazing hindsight is. Everything was much clearer to me now, looking back with my accumulated wisdom and experience. It was not as easy to see the best path back then, faced with different choices, each with its own unique challenges.

With the perspective of hindsight, there are many things I wish I had done differently. However, for each of those things, there is also a reason I am grateful for what I did. There was simply no way to know beforehand what would be effective. Perhaps I kept Kyle at home for too long, isolating him. However, our home program was an illustration of my dedication and commitment to what I believed was right at the time. Maybe it was also an example of my stubbornness, possibly born out of fear. There are always two sides to everything.

Mistakes have turned out to be great teachers, sometimes proving to be even more helpful than "success" would have been. At times, those mistakes spurred new ideas or motivated me to open my mind and explore other options that might benefit Kyle. And, while some of the specific techniques we used didn't really work for him, our attitude of love, acceptance and gratitude became our foundation, infusing all our interactions with gentle compassion. With great love and respect, we strived to give him the "you are doing the best you can" benefit of the doubt. We endeavored to let go of judgments about his behavior and autism as a whole. We looked for things to celebrate, no matter how miniscule, wanting to focus on what was, rather than what wasn't. If I could do things over one hundred times, I would not want to change those things.

Though it's easy to look back and make mental corrections or judgments, I'm not sure how useful this is. In answer to Sarah's question about what I would have done differently, I now believe that wherever I chose to go was where I was meant to be—part of a divine plan I didn't, and don't, control.

A random meeting in a bookstore was a meaningful event on this journey. In helping Sarah, I was able to help myself. Call it coincidence, serendipity, or even divine intervention, it was most definitely a gift.

"It was our last night at the Option Institute, where Gayle and I met. Several of us decided to go out and celebrate. We drove on that cold winter's night on winding mountain roads to one of the local nightclubs in the Berkshires. There were probably about ten of us gathered there, listening and dancing to the music. Gayle, Frank and I danced together, celebrating our week of learning and our newfound friendship."

—*Kathy*

The Essence of Love

Put in My Way

Kathy

I recently saw the movie, "Four Feathers." The central character, Harry, meets a religious man who chooses to be his protector, mentor, and friend. Harry asks the man why? His answer is, "God put you in my way." The religious man believes everything happens according to the will of God, and that Harry was sent to him for a reason.

Mark was sent to me for a reason. He was put in my way. I was on this course of marriage, children, and living life in the so-called "normal" way. And then came Mark.

I awoke. In choosing to be his protector, mentor, and friend, in addition to his parent, I realized quickly that the ways in which I perceived, viewed, and lived my life no longer fit. I resisted, rebelled, yelled, and fought. But in the end, like the oyster and the pearl, I succumbed to what I knew instinctively the first time I saw my son—that I had been given a rare and special gift. I had to change, accept, and adopt new ways that would work for me.

Because of him, I have grown in ways I would never have thought possible. And because of him, I am ten times the person I was when I first started this journey. My heart has grown, as has my vision. Along the way, many people have been there for me when I stumbled, helping me to stand again. I have felt the hand of God on my shoulder directing me every step of the way, even when I denied it was there.

I trust this journey exists for a reason, and has my soul's purpose in hand. I will keep following it until I reach the end, knowing that anything and everything is possible on this quest, because Mark was "put in my way."

The Poem

Gayle

I just read a beautiful article in this month's *Autism Digest* "Inspiration Autism" section. Jennifer Kummins touched my heart with these words: "The poet is the inspired, but the poem is the inspiration. For those people with autism who will become the poets, God bless you. For those people with autism who may, or may not, become the poets, God, the world and I will forever cherish you for being the poem."

We value the poets. We want our children to grow up to be poets. We celebrate them, their achievements, and their perceptible accomplishments. What about the poems?

People like my son are the forgotten poems, easily dismissed as leading lives of less value because they don't fit into the boxes we have created for people. However, it is often the poems that wrap themselves quietly around hearts, altering lives and changing people.

Kyle has impacted the careers, and the ways of living, thinking, and being of those who have formed relationships with him. He has moved people, including his parents, to find places within themselves they didn't know existed. Without talking, without writing, but by the nature of his being, he has altered the world one soul at a time. This is more than many people do in a lifetime.

Each of us yearns to make a difference, to leave our mark on the world. Some of us do this by raising children, having careers, and writing books. Others do this through their essence, without a spoken word. Some are the poets. Some are the poems.

"A week after we met, I decided to give Kathy a call. Since then, we have been talking every Saturday morning for the last fourteen years. This adds up to 336 phone calls, or approximately 40,320 minutes of chat time. I'm convinced these calls have been our secret to staying sane."

—Gayle

Moments of Love

The Kiss

Kathy

Our nighttime rituals are an experience, to say the least. I'm never quite sure how much sleep I'll get because it's often hard for Mark to sleep, and when he's up, I'm pretty much up with him.

I find myself turning off lights, closing the refrigerator door, turning off the television, or if he's watching it, turning the volume down. Puzzles, books, and food are strewn throughout the house. It's like a major, all-night slumber party is taking place, only Mark's the only one who's invited.

Every once in awhile, Mark will call out my name and say goodnight while he's busy at the stove heating something up, or searching for something in the refrigerator. At those times, I've thought about just closing my bedroom door so I won't be disturbed, but then again, he might need me, or if he forgets to turn off the stove, the house would definitely need me!

On one particular night, I was looking forward to going to bed early. Frank, my husband, was out of town on business and I'd cleaned up the dinner dishes earlier than usual. I had finished soaking in the tub and was ready to sink into the nice clean sheets and soft comfortable pillows on my bed. I was even too tired to read, wanting instead just to close my eyes and go to sleep.

My older son, Michael, was at the computer, and Mark was in his room looking at basketball magazines. I said goodnight to each of them, made sure the cats and dog were settled, and climbed into bed.

I had just gotten comfortable when the kitchen light went back on. Our bedroom is off of the kitchen, so every time the light comes on, our room gets really bright. When Mark turns the lights on several times throughout the night, it's like seeing the sunrise over and over again.

I tried to ignore the light and go to sleep, but I noticed Mark had forgotten to close the refrigerator door again. I also heard the TV blaring from his bedroom on the other side of the house. Asking Michael to help wasn't an option. Michael was in bed, and once he's asleep, he's oblivious to any of the commotion Mark creates. The house could be on fire and Michael would sleep through it. So, I got up, figuring it was easier to turn off the light, shut the refrigerator door, and turn down the TV than for Mark to hear me calling him from the other side of the house.

This ritual repeated itself several times throughout this night. Finally, more than a little cranky, and desperately wanting some much needed sleep, I decided that no matter what, I wasn't getting up again.

I settled into bed, and just as I was dozing off, I felt the kitchen light, once again, shining on my face, only this time, I felt Mark's presence near me. He was standing by my bed. I kept my eyes closed, pretending to be asleep. And, just then, he leaned down and kissed me on my forehead. With that kiss, he touched my heart and soul. I might not get a good night's sleep very often, in fact pretty rarely. But that kiss—that moment of love—was worth every lost moment of sleep.

Love Wins

Gayle

Last night was a beautiful, windy, spring evening here in Phoenix, and I was taking a walk with Kyle. He was delighting in watching the trees dance in the breeze to the music of the nearby wind chimes. Every once in awhile, he would stop to stare at a distant light and rapidly shake his head from side to side, producing his own magical light show.

We didn't cover a lot of ground very quickly, but Kyle was enjoying nature and all his self-created sensory wonders. After awhile, I attempted to duplicate his head-shaking motion and discovered what must have been the same visual picture Kyle was enjoying. Due to my own limitations, I couldn't quite move my head as rapidly as he did. I imagine we were an odd sight in the neighborhood.

We were both peacefully enjoying the atmosphere and each other. Now and then, I helped Kyle practice his social referencing skills by incorporating a "stop and go" game into our walk. I have recently come to the point where challenging Kyle doesn't always feel like work, and is more easily interwoven within our moment-to-moment interactions.

Over the years, I have become more adept at slowing down, treasuring the moments, and focusing on each stage as it comes. I know just when I have worked out a strategy or way of coping, Kyle, with his ever-evolving phases, will soon change. During some of the rougher times, this has been a comforting thought. During the more serene times, I wished I could stop the clock.

There have been many times in my life when I've asked myself, God, the universe, and even my doctors, "Why me? Why did this happen to me?" I didn't have time to wait for an answer. So, I got on with the business of adjusting, helping Kyle, and learning all I could about what to do and how to live with what had been a major change in plans. Those questions, however, would still occasionally pop up as I walked the journey of life.

Somewhere along the line, on one of our many walks, I began to consider one possible answer. Kyle came to me to serve as one of my greatest teachers in learning to live well. In his pure innocence, he came here to remind me of what is truly important during my time here on earth. When I listen, and even when I don't, he is here to show me the way. He teaches patience, compassion, creativity, acceptance, authenticity, courage, audacity, and more importantly, the true meaning of love.

It is my love for Kyle that carries me through the difficult moments in life. When I can focus on that true love, I find a deeper peace and happiness.

In the final hour, love wins, and it is Kyle who has shown up to deliver that message over, and over, and over again.

"Gayle's family lovingly refers to our two-hour sessions on the phone as "yak attacks." I call them cheap therapy."

—*Kathy*

Joining the World

Openings

Kathy

Waiting for an "opening" can make the difference between walking through an open door, and running into a closed one. It all depends on what I want to experience—getting in, or getting a big fat headache.

Like today. I'm struggling to write, trying to force myself through a closed door. If it were open, it would be so much easier to get in. The same is true with Mark. When we're working together, it can seem as if all the doors are closed, then suddenly he'll look at me, and I can see that his "door" has opened. I have his attention and go for what I want to teach. Sometimes, I see him struggling to understand something that has been requested of him. Then, the "door" will open, he understands, and is able to proceed. It involves waiting for the right moment, the right time.

I see this in all my relationships. The only way I can reach someone is to wait until that person is open to me. Sometimes, this requires a lot of waiting on my part. Sometimes, I run into a lot of closed doors. Thank heavens Mark gives me lots of opportunities to practice. Not that other people in my life don't, but it's easier for me to see and understand with Mark.

I wait for my own door to open as well. Then I can embrace new ways of doing things. Even when I've persisted in doing something in the same fashion forever, once the light comes on, I can drop the old approach and do things differently.

Within the daily rhythm of our lives, the doors open, and they close. I wait for the moments when they open so I can get in and go for it.

Growth

Gayle

While visiting the school Kyle would be attending, I noticed a young man sitting on the lawn in a squat position. It was the type of squat where your feet are flat, your bottom is almost on the ground, and your chest is resting on your thighs. This teenager was absorbed with the grass in front of him, looking very autistic, and very content. I was struck by this image, because for a moment, I saw the image of Kyle.

Kyle used to sit in this pose. For years, he played, and even ate, in this position. We tried to reach him by placing ourselves below him and gazing into his eyes, or interacting with toys. Sometimes we took this pose with him.

This squat made it possible for Kyle to "fold" inside of himself, to withdraw from the world to a place where he feels safe. For a long time, it was virtually impossible to convince Kyle to sit otherwise.

I don't remember how old Kyle was when he stopped folding himself. Until I saw this young man, I had forgotten Kyle had spent years sitting that way. At some point, Kyle felt safe enough to unfold—to come out and join us in the world. Growth! Or perhaps, his growing legs just got tired.

When did it happen? How could I fail to remember something so significant? Growth sometimes sneaks up on me. It can be big, though often it is tiny. Tiny then *becomes* big. This reminds me that improvement can occur naturally, and not necessarily as a result of an intervention or program. This is where faith comes in.

I strain to recall the time when Kyle unfolded and bloomed. Did I remember to celebrate? If not then, I know I did when I walked past that folded young man who struck the same image Kyle did just years ago.

"Gayle took me hiking on Squaw Peak when I was in Phoenix. She's an avid hiker, unlike her Florida friend. At the top of the mountain, I wondered if the helicopter circling around was for me as I inched my way down the mountain on my backside."

—*Kathy*

Walking in Another's Shoes

Negotiating

Kathy

There is a true art to negotiation, and I use it daily with Mark. I'm getting quite good at it. We both are. I found out early on, that giving him orders or telling him what to do in the usual parental tone, just doesn't work for either of us. All he can hear is my tone of voice, and he wants to move away. Plus, the whole business of bossing someone around just doesn't feel right to me.

So now I make deals. Every time I want something from Mark, whether it's to clean his room, practice his writing, or help me cook, I negotiate with him. I put out what I want, and then he tells me what he wants in exchange. We are dealmakers.

Sometimes we carry it to the extreme. For instance, when I'm talking to my mom on the phone and he wants to talk to her, I give him the phone. Then, when I'm ready to talk again, he negotiates with me to give me the phone back. This might seem crazy, but it works for us.

Looking at this, I realize it is something we all use. We're all making deals, a lot of the time, one way or another. The whole world is a negotiation.

Sometimes it would be easier to go back to the old ways—tell him what to do and be done with it. Coming up with deals is work and requires creativity. There are times when I prefer just to tell him what to do, versus negotiate. But I have found that it feels and works much better when I take the time to make a deal.

I think by working this way, Mark feels a sense of control in a world in which, for the most part, he feels a lack of control. This is good. It doesn't mean I give in to whatever he wants, especially if it's not in his best interest. Rather, we work toward a mutual compromise, something that will make us both happy. Sometimes, it's just about recognizing his need to be recognized as part of the equation.

Negotiation is useful in each of my relationships. Working out deals seems like a much more conducive way of relating to others than ordering, demanding, and insisting things go a certain way. It is a way to respect and honor each of us, while in the process of pursuing what we want. It is definitely worth the effort to practice the "art of negotiation."

Virtual Autism

Gayle

I approached the classroom with apprehension, soon finding myself seated at a desk, wearing a burlap dress. My skin began to crawl, and for a while, I focused exclusively on the scratchy tactile sensations I was experiencing. I became itchy all over and wondered how I was going to endure this assault on my skin over the next hour.

Soon, I could smell strongly scented candles and incense burning throughout the room. In fact, the incense on my desk smoldered toward my face, making my eyes water and my throat dry. It felt like an attack on my olfactory senses, and I couldn't seem to get away from it.

Within minutes, four different types of sound bombarded my ears, each coming from a different corner of the room. Voices, playground noise, music, and other unidentified dissonant sounds, competed loudly for my attention, though I couldn't actually comprehend any of them.

Everywhere I looked, I could see papers on the wall facing in all directions. Most were irrelevant, but eye-catching nevertheless. I didn't know what to focus on first. In the front of the room, people pretending to be a teacher and aide stood speaking in front of a large window. With all this multi-sensory bombardment, I struggled to understand what they were saying.

Soon, they were drilling us with instructions and questions, and at the same time, correcting us for squirming, stretching, or a lack of atten- tion. The questions were coming rapidly. I was unfamiliar with many of the areas they covered, but even when I knew the answers, it was difficult to access them under pressure, amid the sensory overload.

They asked some of us the same question repeatedly. They required we answer something we had already answered ten times in a row, and each time, rewarded us with an unappetizing treat chosen ahead of time by the teacher. The process was frustrating, humiliating, and irritating.

They then told us we would hear a story and be tested on it later. The instructor on the television read the story, but even with the volume all the way up, the story was inaudible. This woman's mouth was moving, but to my ears, no sound was coming out. After about a minute of this, I gave up. I couldn't understand a word, so why give this any further attention? Bored, I began to entertain myself by looking around the room and out the window; every once in awhile, the teacher would prompt me to pay attention.

I had just experienced a slice of the autism world. Just a slice. In contrast to someone with autism, I knew this was just a role-playing experience. I also was fully aware the event would end. I had participated with an intact sensory system (though I had my doubts afterward), and a mind that could rationalize the sensory overload and role-playing activities. Though fully aware I was pretending, I still felt overloaded, overwhelmed, uncomfortable, and a bit frustrated.

I left the room with a headache. My senses had been over-stimulated. My once rational mind was swirling with muddled thoughts and hazy insights. I found myself craving the comfort of sitting in a very quiet room, for a long time.

My compassion rose to new heights. I became keenly aware that I had a tremendous advantage over those with autism who sit in comparable classrooms each day. There's nothing quite like attempting to walk in another's shoes. Though I had often tried to understand Kyle's experience of the world, I had never tasted it quite so powerfully as I did during this role-playing experience. I certainly gained new respect for the immense comfort he derives from rocking in his chair and flapping a piece of paper.

This Virtual Autism class provided one of many eye-openers I experienced during a conference I attended, where I met people who represented the wide spectrum of autism. The challenge of just being and living is so much more profound for these individuals than I had imagined.

As I listened in awe to the speakers with autism, I became aware of the clash between their dreams of fitting in, and their struggle to hang on to their uniqueness. I was impressed with their determination to overcome obstacles, and inspired by their perseverance to seek their dreams, despite prejudice. Gazing through the eyes of compassion, my view of the autism world was forever changed, and for that, I am grateful.

"Each of my three visits to Kathy in Florida has included trips to the beach. One glorious day on the beach, it suddenly became very windy. A bunch of my loose journal pages quickly went flying in all directions. I imagine I was quite a sight running after them."

—Gayle

Smile

So What!

Kathy

One day, Mark started yelling at me. I have no idea why. He wanted me to fix something, but fix what? We struggled with our communication as we tried to reach an understanding.

On another day, we were at the beach and Mark started to have a seizure as we approached the restaurant we like. I looked around to find a quick, safe place to get off the concrete so he wouldn't get hurt if he fell, and get away from people who, while well intentioned, could become more harmful than useful by calling the police or trying to help.

Sometimes we walk into a restaurant or movie where the atmosphere is quiet, and Mark is loud—my Italian-heritage loud. We get the disapproving, "can't you make him be quiet" look from some of the people inside.

On other occasions, well-meaning people will ask, "So what are you doing now that your children are raised?" or "How's your little one doing?" My little one is twenty. Or, those same voices might say, "People like him are so loving and sweet. I know, because my niece is one of them."

And then, there is always my own inner voice—the critic that is ready at a moment's notice to remind me I am lacking, or not good enough to help my son.

Voices, both critical and well intentioned, fill our lives. Most of the time, I can laugh and shrug off these voices. But, there are days when my fuse runs short and I feel defensive, vulnerable, and overwhelmed. Instead of being master at the helm, I feel more like a victim in the boat, being tossed this way and that by a storm that seems to rage in and around me, while I have no direction or control. What do I do? I say, so what!

A friend and mentor from long ago taught me that one of the quickest ways to start feeling good again is to say "so what" and mean it. I feel comfortable using this concept. Instead of being tossed around by the tempest, I can remind myself that even when I seem to be in the midst of the storm's fury, it's no big deal. I can laugh. I can ride the waves and enjoy it. I am honing my skills as a navigator and the sea captain of my life.

As I get stronger with "so what," I notice my personal storm seems to float away, and the rough sea calms down. I know I have just conquered another storm. Blue skies with white clouds reappear. I climb up to my high perch, able to see clearly again. I dust off the debris and seaweed that cling to me, and I smile. I am no longer a victim to my inner voice or the world around me. I am master at the helm, master of me.

Ya Gotta Laugh

Gayle

Kyle and I walked into the restroom. It was, as usual, the women's restroom, because I must accompany him to the lavatory in public places. This has always been the norm and I usually don't think twice about it. Typically, people hear him vocalize or notice his mannerisms and they seem to understand the situation.

On this particular day, we walked into a restroom a few feet behind another woman. From inside the stall, she shouted, "He can't be in here!" As I tried to explain the circumstances, she informed me that he could use the men's room. Abruptly, she stormed out of the stall, giving us an evil look.

At first I was mad, as I sometimes assume the world should automatically accommodate us. "Show some compassion," I snapped. Then I chuckled, wondering if she was going to call the police. I imagined her going back to her office and telling her co-workers the horror story about the odd man with the crazy woman in the ladies room.

In the normal world, a man in the women's restroom must mean trouble, right? However, what if the man is accompanied by his mother? Is he still a threat? It's amazing how insensitive people can be.

When I am out with Kyle, he is sometimes noisy. At times, he makes happy jubilant sounds to express his excitement or pleasure. When he is stressed, he makes more repetitious, anxious vocalizations. Either way, he innocently draws attention to us. I have never liked being the center of attention, and occasionally it feels as if the whole world is my audience.

While they often appear empathetic, people more often seem puzzled or uncomfortable. Many people are not familiar with autism and don't understand the behavior that goes along with it. I would love to carry a business card that says: Don't Worry. It's Just Autism.

One of the best ways I've found to cope when situations occur in public is to maintain my sense of humor. My embarrassment and discomfort diminish when I can see the comical side of Kyle's unusual behavior, and even the reactions of strangers. When I'm at ease, I set an example and others are free to relax. Sometimes, they even smile back.

"Mark has a picture of Gayle he likes. She's half-sitting, half-lying on her couch with the phone to her ear and Leah lying on her chest (when she was little). She sent it to me, even though she doesn't like the way she looks. We were on the phone, during one of our Saturday morning talkfests. I think she looks pretty in her robe, her hair wild and curly, just having awoken from the night before, her daughter close to her. A moment in my friend's life."

—Kathy

Seeing the Possibilities

Beliefs

Kathy

My beliefs are the cornerstone for my work and my time with Mark. What I bring to the table colors everything I do and go for with him. It is important, then, that my beliefs mirror my vision.

I like believing anything and everything is possible. It's all good (whatever the "it" is at the moment). With this belief, I open doors that otherwise would remain closed. For example, I love the beach and wanted to share this with Mark. After doing our program for many years, I took Mark to the beach. He sat in the car, never venturing outside, even for a second. I believed he could enjoy the beach and kept trying. Each time we went, it got a little easier, and today, we walk for miles on the beach. He loves being there and looks forward to the next time we go.

We experienced the same thing with restaurants. At one time, Mark found it impossible to wait to be seated, or even to sit through the entire meal. I wanted him to be able to eat out with us, and believed he could. We kept trying, coaching him and encouraging him until he was able to do it. Today, he loves to eat out.

Our latest goal is teaching Mark to write. I know that once he learns, it will open up a brand new world to him. He'll be able to communicate and express who he is. This is very hard for him. The simple act of holding a pen in his hand and making letters—things we take for granted—are quite challenging for him. Again, I believe he can do this and we work to make it happen. Sometimes I hold his arm so he can get a feel for the way the letter is created. Other times, he watches as I write the letters, and then tries on his own. He is learning. He has mastered many letters. At one time, all he could do was make dots and lines.

Beliefs are the power behind what drives me, so I want them to be a positive force. I was taught that becoming aware of our beliefs is the first step toward changing them. It's kind of like writing. My first draft is often very messy. So, I rewrite until I get to the place where my thoughts are expressed in the best way I can. It's the same thing with my beliefs. My mind is an ocean of rewrites. Every day, I challenge myself to re-create my beliefs so they reflect the kind of world I want for myself, and for those who share it with me.

When I operate under the assumption that something is bad, the world reflects this back to me. For example, if I see autism as bad or hard, I can find plenty of evidence to support this belief. People shower me with tons of well meaning words, or with looks that have me running for shelter quicker than I would from a hailstorm. Or, Mark will do things that have me looking for the nearest cliff.

On the other hand, if I remain open, choosing to see in a way that reflects my positive vision, that, too, is reflected back to me. I can play in the rain, making a game out of dodging the hail, and dance at the edge of the cliff. Those people become my allies and my support, encouraging me at each step. And each thing Mark does is a new opportunity for me to hone in on my skills, becoming the person I was created to be.

My beliefs are my friends or foes, depending on how I create them. Some work for me, the others against. Since I am the author, I choose to write them in a way that works.

Kyle's Angels

Gayle

Last night, Kyle was a wild man! Every so often he has bursts of energy that are extremely challenging to satisfy. He ran laps around the kitchen island, swam for ninety minutes, and concluded the evening by bouncing explosively on his bed. We were both breathless when I tucked him in and hoped he would be able to settle down.

Later on, I tiptoed toward his room to check on him, and much to my surprise, found him in the workout room on the treadmill, trying with all his strength to make it go. Oh my! It was ten o'clock at night and Kyle wanted to run. Time to find those running shoes and get moving. Kyle whipped out twenty-one minutes of interval training—alternately running and climbing steep hills, the sweat pouring off of him, his muscles working to the max. Though I was exhausted and craving sleep, I was delighted he had taken the initiative to get what he needed. I also was in awe as he demonstrated the coordination and focus of a successful athlete on that treadmill. Who would have thought?

To appreciate the magnitude of this, I only needed to remind myself of where Kyle was when he started on this venture.

Enter Kim into our lives, one of Kyle's angels. Kim is Kyle's habilitation therapist, but she is so much more than that. She is a part of our family, almost more like a sister and life coach to Kyle than his therapist. She believes in him, even in the face of everything else. She sees the possibilities and is not afraid to go for them. Often, this has meant pushing Kyle beyond the point he or anyone else thought he could go.

Kim first invited Kyle to step on the treadmill more than a year ago while in her apartment complex workout room. I had never considered it a possibility because Kyle usually doesn't walk more than a few steps without stopping, spinning, or getting distracted. Initially, he was afraid to get on the foreboding machine. For several sessions, Kim would simply ask him to stand on the motionless treadmill. When she eventually turned it on, using the slowest speed possible, she prompted Kyle to take a few steps, and then called it quits. This was the beginning of a long process.

One year later, Kim surprised me. I watched as Kyle walked for ten minutes at one mile per hour. I was astounded and thrilled! Kyle had moved beyond his initial fears, increased his attention span, and improved his physical stamina. Subsequently, we purchased a treadmill for our home. Kyle has improved steadily, regularly walking for thirty minutes at three miles per hour, and sometimes running as fast as five miles per hour.

Since Kim comes from a place of love, she can try almost anything. That's part of being an angel. She believes in Kyle, all the while reassuring him and providing physical and emotional support and encouragement. Loving Kyle, and wanting the best for him, she is willing to go the distance, doing whatever it takes. Sometimes that means pushing past his resistance. At other times, it involves respecting his resistance and backing off. It's a unique dance of intuition and balance.

Thank you, Kim, for giving Kyle the gift of the treadmill, and for inspiring him to learn and grow. Most of all, thanks for continuing to see the possibilities, even in the moments when you were the only one.

~ ~ ~

Note: To Kara, Christy, Patty, Ellen, and all the other past and present angels in Kyle's life (you know who you are), a heartfelt "thank you."

"I get so serious sometimes that when Kathy and I talk, she helps me lighten up. I love that I can be there for Kathy, listen, question, and put my two cents in, helping her to have another perspective."

—*Gayle*

Learning the Lesson

Seizures

Kathy

Mark has had seizures since he was thirteen months old. Throughout the years, his seizures have changed, as one of his doctors said they would. They've gone from little nods of his head, to full-blown episodes incorporating every part of his body. But what has never changed is Mark's attitude toward them.

Mark is so amazing, and such an inspiration to me. I have watched him, and I have watched others watch him, have a seizure. Usually, the pictures are quite different. Mark is accepting of his seizures, never complaining, angry, or attaching any judgments. They just are. He goes with them, wherever they might take him. With others, I often see fear, anger, and a sense of "this is really bad" in their faces. Other times, I see compassion and a desire to help him the best way they can. I guess Mark's seizures tap into our own comfort zones, depending on how we are feeling in the moment—tired, cranky, and fearful, or strong, open, and secure—in the face of new or different situations. It's almost as if he is a vehicle for our life lessons, serving as a good barometer of our own awareness.

A seizure is like an electrical wire that keeps short-circuiting. We have tried many ways to "fix" Mark's seizures so that the "electrical wire" runs smoothly, without short-circuiting. Medications, vitamins, diets, and so on, have led us mostly nowhere. We've come closer by using diet and exercise, and trying to create a stress-free environment.

Mark's seizures remain an ever-present mystery on our journey. We do the best we can, making friends with them in the best way we know how. We trust that Mark has them for a reason, and when the reason is done, the seizures also will be done.

Never having had a seizure myself, I can't imagine what it must be like for him. I don't know how I would act in that situation. But, having watched Mark throughout the years, I would definitely want him as my role model. By his example, he has shown us how to be strong, accepting, open, and courageous. He is love in action.

The Chair

Gayle

There has always been a chair in Kyle's life. Before he was born, we had an old white corduroy rocker-recliner. After his birth, I spent many hours nursing, burping, and cuddling him in that chair. As Kyle grew older, he enjoyed standing on it and rocking vigorously at the same time. Soon, Rachel and Leah arrived and there was more nursing, burping, and cuddling.

Within a few years, the chair began to reach the end of its functional life. The risk of severe structural failure, or the fear of condemnation by the health department, led to its final demise. We also had outgrown it. Kyle was much bigger now, but we were still cuddling as a twosome in this one-person chair.

The next chair we bought was a dark mauve, leather rocker-recliner. Compared to the white chair, this one was king-sized. It also rocked better, so quickly became Kyle's favorite. He spent many, many hours rocking in that chair. It was calming. It also served as an escape, and gave him something to do in a world he often didn't understand. While he enjoyed sitting with other people, he also enjoyed rocking in it alone. The chair was a place of few demands.

At nineteen, Kyle still loves his chair. He now owns the "Hummer" of recliner-rocking chairs—an extra-wide, dark maroon Lazy Boy. Yes, two full-sized adults can sit comfortably in that chair.

Kyle is the master at finding a comfy position while nestled in with someone else. Listening to music, rocking, and watching people are all favorite "chair pastimes." From his chair, Kyle has a good view of the kitchen, hallway, and family room, allowing him to be a quiet observer.

For Kyle, his chair is like an island oasis in a tumultuous sea, a safe haven in the midst of the chaos of life. After a meal, a long day at school, a strenuous workout, or a major change in routine, the chair is always there, reliable and consistent, welcoming him.

Myself, I have had a love-hate relationship with that chair. While I appreciate it for the comfort it offers Kyle, and the break it gives me, the repetitious, solitary activity is very much a symbol of his autism. Sometimes, I feel guilty when I see him sitting there. My conscience says I should be doing something to interact with him, or encourage him to engage in a more productive, functional activity. My judgmental voice asks, "Couldn't he find something more constructive to do?" My grateful self realizes how wonderful it is that he has found a leisure activity so enjoyable and appropriate. I appreciate Kyle's preference and realize he could have many other, less desirable ones.

At times, Kyle uses his leisure activities as means of escape from the world, and the people in it, just like the rest of us. It looks as if his choices express his "different-ness," but in reality, I realize how alike we are. I do envy the ease with which he slips into a relaxation mode. I am reminded of how much I cherish my own escape time.

Kyle has latched onto a treasure—a solid place in our wobbly, unpredictable world. In "the chair," he has learned to create peace for himself. How nice.

"At the end of the year, Gayle and I like to share our New Year's resolutions with each other. In the beginning, our lists were small and easy to achieve. As the years went by, our lists became bigger and bigger, so much so, it took all of our energy and time just to read them, much less do them. Such was our enthusiasm and excitement. We've since learned to keep them small and doable."

—*Kathy*

Heal Thyself

Honoring Our Differences

Kathy

One night, while the four of us were having dinner at a favorite Chinese restaurant, we ran into an old friend. I noticed when she said hi to Mark, she talked to him as if he were still four years old, his age when she last worked with him in our home-based program. It felt weird. Mark is now an adult. I then realized many people respond to him this way, even Frank, Michael, and me.

This incident reminded me of the way people talk to the elderly, or those who've had strokes—as if they are very young children. We assume they can't understand. Are we doing the same thing to Mark?

Sometimes, we've talked about him as if he weren't in the room. Because he doesn't respond like we do, we've carried on conversations without him, or talked to him as if he were a very young child, instead of the adult he is. I know it's because he doesn't communicate in the same way we do.

I believe we don't intend to be mean or disrespectful, even though, like our friend in the restaurant, it can come off that way. Our behavior stems from our lack of awareness. Now that I am aware, I choose to do things differently. I've changed the way I relate to my son, and others as well. I no longer make assumptions about what he understands, and instead give him the benefit of the doubt. I include him whenever possible, even if he can't respond in kind. I extend this same level of respect to others as well.

By making these changes, I create new bridges and opportunities for us to communicate. By reaching out, I cross the bridge of isolation in hopes of connecting with this very special person, and every other person I encounter. By honoring Mark in this way, I give him the respect he deserves, and grow in my own ability to communicate with the people in my world. Even if words should get lost in the process, my attitude won't. And that is more important than anything I might have to say.

Mirrors

Gayle

People are like mirrors, reflecting back to us our own, imperfect selves.

Qualities and behaviors we dislike in others often resemble the very things we dislike about ourselves.

I became acutely aware of this recently when I noticed how some of my relatives and acquaintances treat Kyle. The way they interact with him, or rather, *don't* interact with him, speaks volumes about their uneasiness. Maybe, out of their own fears of rejection or inadequacy, they are afraid to try. Perhaps his very existence forces them to face uncomfortable feelings.

Now, here's the mirroring part. I am doing the same thing with my autistic brother, Philip. I have ignored Philip most of his life. As his legal guardian, I attend the necessary meetings, but I have not pursued a relationship with him. It's been easier not to invest the emotional energy and time, and has lessened the potential for pain or discomfort. Out of sight, out of mind.

My mother did the same thing. For most of her life, she pretended he didn't exist. It was too painful for her. She never got to know her son, and he never got to know his mother.

Our family didn't talk much about Philip. In fact, for many years, I didn't even know what he had. Growing up, there was so much physical and emotional distance between us, I was essentially an only child. In essence, I still am.

So, now I ask myself, do I want to go through the remainder of my life just doing my job as Philip's legal guardian? Or, do I want to have a real relationship with my brother? I want to have a real relationship with my brother.

I believe I am ready. At first, Philip might be indifferent to my efforts, and it could feel awkward. I will need to move through the clumsiness and discomfort to create the connection. I just need to take one step at a time and not let my fears dissuade me. After the first step, the next one should be easier. It's what I want for myself, and for Philip.

I know I am an example for my daughters, constantly modeling action and inaction. I pray Rachel and Leah do not ignore their brother as I have mine. I want Kyle to be a part of their adult lives in whatever way they choose. I do not want him to be the non-person on the periphery. I am altering the attitude and behaviors passed on to me by my mother. In some ways I already have, by the way I perceive and treat Kyle. I am now ready to take things to the next level.

Gazing into the mirror, so many reflections stare back at me—images of the past with my mother and brother, the present with my relatives and friends, and the future with my daughters. We are all reflections of each other, mirroring our strengths and weaknesses, the richness of who we are.

Clockwise from left: Rachel, Gayle, Neil, Leah, & Kyle Nobel

Clockwise from left: Frank, Michael, Kathy, & Mark Almeida

Leah, Neil, & Rachel Nobel

Kyle Nobel & Kim (his friend)

Michael & Mark Almeida

Frank & Kathy Almeida

Gayle & Kathy,
February 18 to 22, 1991,
the week we met

Gayle & Kathy,
April 2004

Kyle, 6 months

Kyle, 3 (center)

Kyle, 21

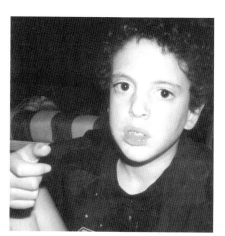

Kyle, 9

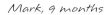
Mark, 9 months

Mark, 2 (center)

Mark, 21

Mark, 9

Gayle & Kyle, 2

Gayle & Kyle, 22

Kathy & Mark, 6

Kathy & Mark, 21

Gayle, January 2006

Kathy, February 2006

"*I love our Saturday morning talks. We discuss our guys and all the things that came up for us that week. Then, we get to other important stuff, like what to do with our wild and outrageous curly hair.*"

—*Gayle*

The Gift of Now

Seafaring

Kathy

In May, Frank, Michael, Mark, and I, went away for twelve days, making our way up the eastern coast toward Nova Scotia, our final destination. We stayed in the quaint town of Bar Harbor, Maine, with plans to take the ferry to Nova Scotia the following day. Our time was limited, so taking the ferry would give us a taste of the country without having to sit for the full meal.

Bar Harbor is nestled in a small sea cove surrounded by mountains. We enjoyed our night there, eating at one of the local taverns, and stopping in the shops as we walked along the city sidewalks. Our ferry, "Cat," sat docked in the harbor among many other boats.

Now, for the record, I have not been the world's best seafarer. In fact, at that time, my sea legs had yet to be born, so every time I got on a boat, I got sick. The good news was, "Cat" was new and could make the trip in three hours, versus eight on the old boat.

So, the next day, after parking our car on the deck below, we went upstairs to a really nice deck of plush chairs and eating areas. It even had a place to gamble if you desired. We met another couple that assured me the ride was very smooth and I would be fine. So much they knew. As soon as the boat started to move out of the dock, I instantly felt sick. Frank said I looked green. I made my way to the bathroom where, for the next twenty minutes or so, I became best friends with one of the portables.

Eventually, when I had progressed to dry heaves, I decided the movement in the bathroom was worse than where my men were located, so I wobbled safely back and lied down on the floor next to Frank, who reclined in one of those plush, comfortable chairs. I closed my eyes, praying for the ship to stop, or the ocean to still, but with each wave, I felt my body shudder and the nausea reemerge.

I prayed for the hours to become minutes and the three-hour track to end in a heartbeat. Looking at me, Michael said he guessed it wasn't all in my head after all. If I could have moved, I would have decked him. But, the only response I could give was to breathe without heaving.

In the midst of all of this, I became aware of something new. Every time we approached a new wave, I would prepare my body by flinching, getting ready to fight the movement. I realized that when I resisted, trying to protect myself, I felt even worse than before. So I decided to use a concept I had heard of—"going with" the movement, versus fighting it. With the next wave, instead of putting my body in fight mode, I relaxed. Something exciting happened. Even though I still didn't feel like dancing, I wasn't throwing up. So, for the next two and a half hours, that's what I did. I focused on going with the movement and relaxing my body, instead of fighting each rolling motion of the boat.

This experience taught me how important it is to relax and go with the flow. Mark, my resident teacher, presents me with lots of opportunities to use this technique. When he resists trying something new, instead of pushing him, I relax and wait. If he doesn't want to clean up his room, I relax and come up with ways to motivate him rather than force the issue. If he forgets to close the refrigerator door, instead of yelling at him, I relax and remind him to close it. The list goes on.

My brother says everyone has a distinct function in life. He says mine is to feed the fish. Funny. But, I think all that "chumming" also might have provided me with this same lesson—to go with the flow. Chumming is a tedious task, but by being in the moment, I learned what works, and what doesn't.

From the seafaring, chumming, and most importantly, the work with my son, I have learned to relax and "go with." Compared to fighting and resisting, "going with" feels a lot better. And as a result, I have grown my sea legs.

Reflections on Twenty

Gayle

Kyle turned twenty years old today, also marking my twentieth year as a mom. It has certainly been a turbulent, unanticipated journey.

During Kyle's first year, we experienced his out-of-control seizures, multiple medication changes, and delayed development. As time went by, Kyle slid further and further behind. Initially, we didn't realize the extent of his challenges. A multitude of tests and evaluations were followed by years of various therapies. We spent what felt like centuries in our special playroom, attempting to enter Kyle's world and inviting him over the imaginary bridge into ours. We controlled his seizures with the aid of alternative medicine. While there were times of little or no progress, we always persevered.

Just as we were riding along on our rocky, yet stable road, puberty showed up. Although many children go through a certain amount of difficulty during puberty, this hormonal onslaught upset Kyle's fragile stability. Puberty seemed to trigger some severe and very intense episodes of anxiety.

These episodes came in two-week cycles. During those two weeks, Kyle would become a completely different person. When the two weeks ended, he would revert back to being himself as if nothing had ever happened. Suddenly, we were dealing with something very foreign to us. What was happening to our happy, easygoing boy?

During these cycles, Kyle would be in a near constant state of distress and agitation. He had difficulty eating, and his comforting habits and routines were no longer helpful. In fact, he seemed to have forgotten all about them. It was almost impossible to do anything with him. The goal became survival. We focused on getting through each day trying to convince him to eat and helping him get comfortable. These were some of the most frightening and frustrating times for our family. They certainly challenged me enormously to maintain the attitude of acceptance I had been cultivating over the years.

We experimented with dietary interventions, more alternative medicine, and even drugs, all in an attempt to control these episodes. Some helped for a while. Many times, just when we were convinced we had these episodes whipped, they would reappear.

These cycles went on for many years until Kyle hit the magic age of eighteen, and then they stopped. Had the hormones suddenly leveled out, or had Kyle just adjusted to them? Had we found the magic antidote in the antifungal medication? Almost inexplicably, Kyle moved past the anxiety to settle into his late teens. We all breathed a big sigh of relief.

Now, twenty years into my journey as a mother, I have reached an important passage. I worked very hard during the last twenty years to be an extraordinary mom to my extraordinary son. Though I still have many dreams for Kyle and our relationship, I feel at ease with my circumstances.

I do hang on to dreams of knowing and understanding Kyle better, of having a relationship with him that doesn't require such hard work, and of watching him participate and enjoy life more fully. I also accept what is. This is the tricky part, and might seem contradictory since the typical way of thinking is to be dissatisfied so one can want something more or better. Dissatisfaction is then used to justify desire. I believe it is possible to want something passionately, and still accept and even love what is with equal passion. Wanting more does not diminish what I have.

I have discovered I can hold on to my dreams for the big picture *and* celebrate the accomplishments of each day. I can relate to Kyle with the attitude that he is fine as he is (yes, unusual behavior, and even anxiety episodes), while keeping my dreams tucked away in my pocket.

I can use the light of my dreams to illuminate the beauty and wonder that exists directly in front of me.

"Gayle and I were hiking up a mountain and got caught in a huge thunderstorm. I told Gayle lightning strikes the tallest thing in the area. She then proceeded to lie down on the wet ground, saying, "I'm small, I'm small." Looking at her, I forgot to be scared and laughed until it hurt."

—Kathy

Nourishment for Body and Soul

Food

Kathy

I used to see food as a major issue for Mark. Now, I see it has been an amazing opportunity for all of us.

When we first became aware of Mark's autism and seizures, one of the first things we looked at was his diet. We've always thought the choice of food was connected to his well-being. Actually, it affects everyone's, but particularly his since he is more sensitive than we are. We noticed that when he ate certain things, he'd have more seizures, and the seizures would change in intensity. His eyes would look drugged, and he'd be more lethargic and less able to talk. His behavior also would change. Sometimes he would become extremely hyperactive. His moods would shift from sweet, to not so sweet.

As we became more aware of the effects of different foods on Mark, we changed our diets to do whatever we could to help him. When we realized how many chemicals animals were fed, we became vegetarians. Today, we remain vegetarians, not only for health reasons, but also for the animals' welfare.

We also wanted to eliminate from our diets any foreign substances that might contribute to Mark's overall condition, so we stopped eating processed foods and most junk foods because of the additives used to either enhance the flavor of the food or extend its shelf life. We switched from the "whites" to the "browns," (flour, sugar, and rice), and started using organic foods whenever possible to avoid pesticides. We began eating raw and fresh cooked vegetables over canned to get the freshest possible food. These changes not only have helped Mark, but we're all healthier, getting fewer colds and "non-existent" viruses than we used to get.

Mark's allergies to certain foods also have challenged me as a cook. Throughout the years, he has been allergic to many foods including sugar, wheat, dairy, soy, citrus, and the foods in the nightshade family. As a result, I often cook two different meals for dinner. I make one "user friendly" meal for Mark, and one for the rest of us. Otherwise, it's way too expensive to cook solely for his diet. But, for the most part, I try to find foods that will work for all of us.

On this journey to find "safe food," I have discovered many new foods and ways of cooking. Because I love to cook, our holidays, traditions, and even everyday celebrations like TGIF (Thank Goodness It's Friday), revolve around dinner. I want our food not only to nourish our bodies, but also our souls. It's an ongoing quest I enjoy—one that challenges my skills and creativity. There have been plenty of "throw-aways" in the process. One time I baked a cake without wheat, dairy, sugar, or eggs. I think Michael was the only one brave enough to eat it.

We certainly have had our issues with all of this. In addition to resisting the changes, we've spent a lot of energy trying to keep Mark away from the so-called "forbidden foods." He wanted to eat what we ate and couldn't have. It became a tug of war, with me playing police guard or nice guy. Often the answer was to just eliminate the food in question so it was no longer an issue, although that wasn't always an option.

What I've come to know and appreciate is that, as with most things, attitude is everything. Overreacting, getting angry, or acting out in fear when he chooses "bad" foods, only adds more stress to an already stressful situation. Having a relaxed attitude works much better when I am encouraging him to choose foods that support him, versus those that don't.

Restaurants are a challenge. It used to be hard to find restaurants that served vegetarian foods. Not anymore. The challenge now is to find a place that caters to someone with food sensitivities like Mark's. We have found that Chinese and Thai restaurants seem to work the best. Another option is to have a picnic. We have brought our own food on trips, or to the beach. Being outside is fun, relaxing, and it works!

These changes have been worth it for each of us. We are healthier, and more importantly, we understand the role diet plays in Mark's well-being. It's the difference between night and day. When he eats foods that support him, he is more easily able to participate and be a part of our world. And that is worth every bit of work we do to get there.

Food

Gayle

Kyle has always been passionate about food. As a toddler, when we had his hearing evaluated, he didn't respond to the sound of his name, but consistently turned to the word "cookie." Practically from the time he could chew, he was a lover of buttered rye toast.

When Kyle was three, we decided to consider alternative medicine. He was taking three anticonvulsants, experiencing debilitating side effects, and still having twenty seizures a day. It seemed we had nothing to lose when we visited our first homeopathic physician. He created a series of custom remedies for Kyle and suggested I make changes in his diet. This was the first time I had even considered food might affect his neurological health. In hindsight, the changes he suggested were very modest, though at the time, they seemed monumental.

Eighteen years later, Kyle remains consistently seizure free. We never determined whether food affected his seizure activity. However, the homeopathic remedies eventually helped stop the seizures, allowing us to discontinue three of the medications and reduce the remaining one.

When Kyle was fifteen, we were looking for a way to help relieve his incapacitating, cyclical anxiety episodes without using heavy medication. I was referred to a doctor who specialized in environmental medicine. After a long series of allergy tests, he determined Kyle was sensitive to an extensive list of foods. In addition to eliminating the culprits, he also advised us to rotate the remaining foods. Admittedly, I met these suggestions with fear and resistance, feeling as though our world had been turned upside down. It was difficult to imagine Kyle's life without rye bread or pizza, but I was determined to give the new diet a try.

In the beginning, the diet felt like a burden because I often ended up fixing two different meals for the family. But, as time went by, I became more organized. I found simple solutions to reduce my burden, such as cooking Kyle's rice noodles alongside the family's wheat pasta.

Since Kyle couldn't have eggs or potatoes for breakfast every day, I served baked turnips as an alternative in the four-day rotation. Kyle usually accepted this, since turnips, if sliced thinly, doused with olive oil and garlic salt, and baked until extra crispy, almost pass for potato chips. Except for the smell. Pretty soon, Rachel and Leah were begging me to never fix turnip crisps again. (I got the same reaction to fish, although I never made that for breakfast.)

Kyle was a good sport about the new diet, and even learned to like many things he had not eaten before. His passive nature made it easy for me to be consistent. He didn't raid the refrigerator, and while he might bring me a loaf of contraband bread (his way of asking for it), he easily accepted substitutions.

We discovered that food did indeed seem to have an impact on his anxiety episodes. When we first began the diet, the episodes stopped for many months. After awhile, he began to have some breakthrough episodes that responded to an antifungal medication. Indirectly, the anxiety still seemed to be food related.

In addition to cupboard adjustments, I made many attitude adjustments along the way. Throughout the process, I found I had to make a conscious decision to be open-minded, choosing to believe I could do anything I set my mind to. I sought the support of people who would encourage me. Even though I was a vegetarian, I set aside some of my beliefs when I discovered the diet was much more doable if I added meat to the rotation. It quickly became apparent that Kyle adored meat and could enjoy it without the adverse reaction he had to pizza.

It has been tempting to fall into the trap of blaming food for nearly every behavior or anxiety issue. It's easy to make food the bad guy when you want to feel a sense of control and crave a solution. Over the years, I've learned it usually isn't that simple. A variety of factors are involved.

I can drive myself crazy worrying about which food might be affecting Kyle in a particular situation. It's easy to have tunnel vision and forget that, like anyone, he could be out of sorts for no apparent reason. Though food is a factor for Kyle, it is not the only factor. On any given day, food can be the demon or the good guy.

Kyle is healthier and happier without the presence of certain foods in his diet. In many ways, the same is true for me. Mealtime remains one of Kyle's favorite moments of the day. I am grateful that through perseverance, I have discovered a relatively simple way to improve the quality of Kyle's life, and in turn, ours as well.

"Kathy always seems to be baking something while we talk. I can almost smell the aroma of her wheat-free blueberry muffins coming through the phone. I marvel at how she manages to do it."

—*Gayle*

Fitting In

Normal

Kathy

I live in a world of "normal." When it's not normal, I try to make it so. I guess I've been trying to do that ever since I found out Mark was different. It's strange. I have always been a champion for anything that was different. I can live in a world loving all that God has created, finding wonder in each and every thing, and yet still be so influenced by the society in which I live.

The hardest part has been constantly smacking into the reality of society's dynamics. A lot of times, it just doesn't work for Mark to be involved in what's happening. Still, I don't like it when anyone I love is excluded or left out. You'd think I'd be over this by now, but I still have difficulty at times.

I strive to live in a world where it works for all of us—where we all fit and are welcomed, accepted and loved, just as we are. I want to live in a world where people don't ask if your son is still making progress. Who asks that question of a "normal" child? It's like a dagger that finds its way into my heart, reminding me that even when I think we might fit in, we're still on the outside of the loop.

I think this is part of the reason I have tried so hard for all these years to make things "right"—to fit in. But, underneath it all, I see that I wanted something more.

It's like someone wanting to live on a street where all the houses are brick, everyone drives a brand new Suburban, and the kids are all graduating from college and going on to white-collar jobs. This is one way of thriving in a society based on its measures of success. But, while this street is good, it's just one in a world filled with many different types of streets. Life is so much bigger than trying to fit into "one" way. I remind myself of this whenever I start to compare our lives, or get caught up in being normal.

Our life is like our home, set apart on lots of land of rolling hills and wide-open spaces. This is good, too. I'm free to let go of my need for normal, and relish and enjoy the beauty and uniqueness of my own street.

Get Out of the Graveyard

Gayle

On the day of Kyle's eighteenth birthday, we happened to have a brief encounter with Kyle's aunt. Kyle was getting into the car when she looked at him with sorrowful, pitiful eyes, and exclaimed, "How sad! He should be out driving, having girlfriends and working. I wish this hadn't happened to him." "Get out of the graveyard," I replied. "That's not who he is. In essence, you are saying you wish he were someone else." How sad I felt for her. In eighteen years, she still didn't know Kyle, and probably continued to see him as unreachable, and perhaps incapable.

Later on, I regretted my response, which probably seemed to come out of nowhere. That was most likely not what she had meant by her comments, but rather my interpretation, based on how I viewed Kyle and his autism.

I realized I might have played an indirect role in her prolonged state of mourning over Kyle, and the expected "normal" that never came. I had isolated Kyle from our extended family. I had wanted to make things easier for Kyle by surrounding him with those who were comfortable with him, and supportive of me. I spent many years keeping him out of the real world.

Now, when Kyle goes out into challenging community and social situations, I see that he rises to most occasions and adapts well. The world is also beginning to make room for him.

Sometimes, I think the grief and sadness someone might feel over a loved one's autism creates a fog that obscures his ability to get to know the autistic person, or develop a relationship with him. Jim Sinclair, a man with autism, wrote: "You didn't lose a child to autism. You lost a child, because the child you waited for never came into existence. We need and deserve families who can see us and value us for ourselves, not families whose vision of us is obscured by the ghosts of children who never lived. Grieve if you must, for your own lost dreams. But don't mourn for us."

At some point, we must all get out of the graveyard. I recognize this is an uncomfortable proposition for many. I can look at Kyle through the eyes of others and understand how they might not know how to relate to him. Sinclair wrote: "Yes, it takes more work than relating to a non-autistic person. But it can be done—unless non-autistic people are far more limited than we are in their capacity to relate. We spend our entire lives doing it. Each one of us, who manages to reach out and make a connection with you, is operating in alien territory. And then *you* tell *us* that we can't relate."

Could it be that the world is as "disabled" as the disabled? I chuckle as I envision a whole parking lot full of handicap spaces.

"One morning, on our Smoky Mountain trip, Gayle and
I sat on the balcony of our rented condo and I taught her
how to make an Appalachian egg basket. I love to make
baskets, and Gayle was an eager student. We laughed
and talked as we worked our fingers, weaving in and
out, in tune with the rhythm of the mountain stream
below with basket reed strewn all around us."

—Kathy

First Do No Harm

Our Dentist Days

Kathy

Yesterday, I took Mark to the dentist in Gainesville, which is about an hour's drive from where we live. We enjoyed traveling north on I-75, listening to music and looking at the scenery passing by.

I used to get really nervous about taking Mark to the dentist. First, I worried about being in the reception area, wondering if he would be able to wait his turn. Then, I worried about how he would act, and what the other people in the waiting room would do—stare disapprovingly, or be open and friendly.

I worried about the actual appointment and how I would get Mark to sit in the dentist chair, open his mouth, and let some stranger with a facial mask and lots of metal tools work, while one little hose sprayed water into his mouth, and another sucked it out. Not knowing if the whole procedure made any sense to him, I prayed he wouldn't bite the dentist's hand from fear and misunderstanding. When x-rays were necessary, I would explain the procedure and show him what was expected. Still, it wasn't easy for him. Usually by the end of the visit, I would be a bundle of nerves and have a major headache.

Mark has visited the dentist since he was little. During Mark's early days at the dentist, he was drugged and his hands were strapped to the armrest so the dentist could work on Mark's teeth without interruption or problems. I can remember Mark looking at me, saying, "all stuck," referring to his hands. Even now, I feel guilty for allowing that to happen.

On the way home from those visits, Mark would get very nauseous. I would hold his head while he threw up out the window, so he wouldn't fall out, all while I was driving. It seems like just yesterday.

We tried other dentists. They were better, but still had no patience or respect for his special needs.

A few years back, Mark and Michael both needed their wisdom teeth removed. I prayed it would be an easy experience for Mark, knowing the whole thing could throw him off. It was an easy experience, but only for Michael. Mark had pain—excruciating pain and discomfort. He wanted me to "fix it," to make the pain go away. Teasingly, I begged the doctor to give *me* drugs, so I could sleep until Mark felt better. It would have been nice if both of us could have magically slept through to the healing, but, alas, that wasn't to be. In addition to the pain of the extractions, he bit his lip until it turned into a bloody pulp. Numbed by the Novocain, his lip felt weird to him. When the effects of the Novocain subsided, his lip looked like it had been through a war.

As a result of these experiences, the first time we walked into our current dentist's office, Mark was terrified and screamed. I think he was afraid the "wisdom teeth" occurrence would happen again. It took several visits for him to realize this wasn't the case.

Today, our trips to the dentist are totally different. We have a great dentist. Everyone is friendly and nice to us. They welcome Mark, asking him if "everything is going to be alright?" This is his favorite greeting. Mark befriends everyone in the waiting room. The dental hygienist is respectful and patient with him. She gives him time to get in the chair and lay his head back for his cleaning and examination, and explains everything to him while she's doing it. They are all supportive and nurturing of me as well.

Whenever we go, it feels as if we have come home to people who love and care about us. I am so grateful for these people. Who would have thought a dentist's office could be like this? Not me. Not after what we'd experienced. I realize now how comfortable and relaxed I felt being there. I don't worry, and Mark does great. What a difference.

We've both come a long way. What used to be a dreaded, but necessary, event, is now a fun day's outing. Pretty amazing.

Beneath the Veil

Gayle

Quite some time ago, our pediatrician informed us it was time to take Kyle to a doctor who treats adults. If it were up to me, I would stay with our pediatrician forever. Having treated Kyle since early infancy, he knows our story and is great with both of us. We've had a successful working relationship throughout the years, and it is with reluctance that we make a change.

How do I begin with a new doctor? How can I tell him our twenty-year saga in a fifteen-minute office visit? What does he really need to know about Kyle, and what do I want him to discover for himself?

As with everyone, I hope he can learn to look beneath the veil. This can be a challenge, even for me. In one respect, given Kyle's regular appearance, it's hard to imagine the extent of his challenges. However, beneath his perfect physical features, sensory disarray can make his world a positively overwhelming place.

The body of my strong, tall, twenty-year-old acts as a veil for an emotional self that could really be very young. I want our new doctor to approach Kyle as a young man, and at the same time remember there is a little person inside who might be very frightened and unable to understand what's happening. I want him to be compassionate toward him without babying or talking down to him.

Often, the first thing people seem to notice is Kyle's unusual behavior. They might not even notice he looks the same as you and me, instead paying more attention to his humming, vocalizing, or flapping.

His actions lead them to believe there isn't much going on inside. They easily underestimate the extent of his understanding and awareness.

After going to an autism conference recently, attended by many non-verbal people who were achieving at the college level, I began reminding myself that I want to assume more competence in Kyle. This is what I'd like from others as well. Since relationships in our society are based very much on verbal connections and unspoken social rules, where does a nonverbal person like Kyle, who lacks understanding of those rules, fit in? Is he to live forever as an observer on the periphery of life? Sometimes I have no answers, only questions.

So, after procrastinating for months about this transition to a new doctor, we finally opted to see my sister-in-law's long-time family practice physician. During our first office visit, I was relieved to see he didn't push Kyle too much beyond what he was willing to tolerate during the examination. It was evident he didn't want to force himself on Kyle. He patiently examined him with a respectful, gentle kindness. While he'd had no experience with someone with autism, he entered the relationship with an open mind, and perhaps an open heart. What more could I ask?

"I absolutely love Kathy's baskets. I have many in different sizes and colors around my house. I was excited to learn how to make one. There wasn't enough time for me to finish my creation so I carried it on the plane along with all the materials to finish it at home. For about four years, it sat in my closet calling out to be finished. I eventually ended up with a basket, and after all that time, I even remembered how to make it."

—Gayle

Appearances Can Be Deceiving

Persistence

Kathy

Last week, I watched a television program about a woman who is able to break through the barriers caused by her son's autism and communicate with him. She is able to ask him about anything, and he is able to reply through writing and by using his computer. When asked what he thought was the biggest misconception about autism, he said people assume those with autism don't understand anything, and that's not true. They do understand. When you think they're not getting it, they are.

I am inspired by the boy's statement, and by his mother's persistence. His mother never quit, even when he resisted. She practiced with him over and over again until he got whatever it was they were working on. This mother and son showed me that, yes, Mark does hear me, and, yes, it is possible for him to learn, even when he resists and puts up his defenses. All I need to do is believe in him, be persistent, and break the lesson down into small, doable steps.

In the past, I have let his resistance throw me off many times. I took it to mean either he wasn't interested, or it was too hard. Yet, I now realize that when I pay attention, he shows me he is learning and is understanding.

I could go on and on listing all the things Mark has learned when nobody thought he was watching. The other day, Frank and Michael were playing basketball. It seemed as if Mark wasn't paying attention to what they were doing. However, after they'd finished and gone on to something else, Mark picked up the ball and started shooting hoops and making the shots. At times, when I thought he wasn't looking, I've hid food I didn't want him to eat. Later, he would go right to it. There also have been times I've asked him to do something, like bring food scraps to the cows, and he did it.

I might have given up too easily in the past, thinking that what I was doing wasn't working, when all I needed to do was spend a little more time doing things step by step. No matter. That was then and this is now. I am inspired to start again. I want to be able to totally communicate with Mark. I want him to be able to freely write and speak his thoughts. I believe it is possible, and now I know the key is persistence. This time, we're both up for the challenge.

Connections

Gayle

After being sick for a week, Kyle rebounded by having an amazing three days. I was delighted and excited, wishing I could freeze the moments, making them last forever.

There was an awareness and attentiveness about Kyle I don't often see. At times, it was almost magical. Kyle was very active, but not hyperactive or out of control. He appeared more interested in people and his surroundings than usual. He wasn't attracted to his routine, repetitious activities. Several times, I found him just standing in his room, or in the hallway, waiting for something to happen with a distinct and unusual clarity, alertness, and focus. He seemed more organized, his neurological system allowing him to follow through on routines with ease.

I find these times fascinating and mysterious. I have created visual images—metaphors—to help me understand something I find baffling. Kyle's mind reminds me of an electrical cord plugged into an outlet. When he is "on," it's as if the synapses in his brain are connecting and firing fully. The cord is plugged in and the current is powerful, strong, and continuous. Kyle is able to perceive the world more clearly because many of the riots and distractions that normally fill his brain are quiet.

I imagine during other, more typical, times, his brain is filled with static. While it is plugged in, the electrical cord is not completely pushed into the socket. It's loose and jiggling around so the connection is sometimes complete and sometimes not there at all, but most often is fuzzy and irregular. The connection comes and goes like a radio signal fading in and out, mixed with interference.

What must it be like to experience the world through Kyle's senses? In the blink of an eye chaos replaces calmness. The patterns he relies on are abruptly removed. Trying to make sense out of it all, he seeks familiarity, sameness, and consistency in a world that is spinning rapidly around him.

Yesterday morning, when Kyle awoke, the plug was almost completely free of the outlet. I could see that the prior days' connection had vanished. Here was a Kyle who didn't quite have his act together. This became apparent right away when I noticed the look in his eyes, heard the sounds he was making, and observed the way he navigated through his morning routine. The window of opportunity experienced during the prior days appeared closed.

We all have our off days. Nobody is completely consistent each day, though Kyle's ups and downs are often more extreme. It's as if someone keeps tripping over that electrical cord and disengaging it. Often, I look for a reason for the variations. Was it something we did? A food he ate? The weather? An illness or allergy? The full moon? Rarely do I have any answers. On any given day, the plug will engage and the window of opportunity will again present itself.

I realize that if I am to exist happily and peacefully, I must strive to live more in the present moment, learning to love the times when the plug is loose and the cord is dangling. Anyone can delight in the extraordinary moments. I strive to embrace the more challenging times that bring the tougher lessons. It is an ongoing process.

Each morning, I wake up to a surprise at the other end of the house. It is Kyle's ever-evolving way of being. One day at a time, we both grow and transform. Kyle takes on his challenges with amazing grace. As for me, I strive to do the same.

"I always feel comforted, inspired, and light-hearted when Kathy and I talk. I'm not even sure how or why, but I do. It's just a fun time. We usually wind up laughing about something."

—Gayle

Miracles

A Dream Coming to Meet Me

Kathy

I remember how, many years ago, I would sit and look outside the window of the special room we created for Mark, and while working with him, dream of the day we could be out there, living our lives like everyone else.

Yesterday was one of those days when my dream came to meet me.

It was Sunday, a gorgeous spring day. The four of us took off for Tampa and St. Pete, a two and a half hour drive from our home, give or take. I wanted to take my guys to this bridge in Tampa my sister had shown me. It's an old bridge over Tampa Bay that has since been closed to cars. It's now a pedestrian walkway. People walk, ride bikes, skate, and run on it. There's also a place to fish.

Before we walked the Tampa Bridge, we went to St. Pete. We drove across the new bridge and around the city, stopping for lunch at one of the local restaurants. The food worked out for all of us—it was vegetarian, and user-friendly for Mark. After lunch, we parked by the bayside and walked around the marina and the park. The sky was clear and the blue water of the bay reflected onto the surrounding buildings. It was cool—not humid and sticky like summer—with a nice breeze. The boats in the harbor glistened from the suns rays. The seagulls flew overhead, making their presence known by squawking loudly. People sat on park benches, rode bikes, and jogged. Some sat on blankets near the water's edge. A sports event had just finished and the workers were taking down the bleachers and the white tents. We took all of this in as we walked, and then sat on one of the benches, enjoying this day.

Next, we went to Gandy Bridge to walk across it. Frank was busy taking pictures of the scenery, while Michael, Mark and I walked and enjoyed looking over the bridge. Sailboats, pontoon boats, and motorboats all dotted the landscape in front of us. Airplanes flew overhead, so low you felt as though you could reach up and touch one. To the east lay the city of Tampa, outlining the coast. We watched as the setting sun illuminated the sky in bright orange and red. It was a beautiful day, and a miracle for us.

To be able to have a day like this was special. There was a time this would not have worked for Mark. Sitting in a restaurant, walking around the park and on the bridge, following the social rules we take for granted, focusing and connecting with us—none of that would have worked. Today it did, all of it.

He has come so far. We were a family enjoying a normal Sunday outing. The dream I had sent out that window so long ago had come to meet me. I am blessed.

The Wedding

Gayle

Kyle recently attended Kara's wedding. If anyone had told me a few years ago this would be possible, I might not have believed it.

Kara is a very special person. In a sense, I've watched her grow up since she was sixteen and began volunteering with Kyle. Ten years later, she was getting married and wanted Kyle to attend the wedding. She was enthusiastic about including Kyle in her special event. A year prior, Kara had escorted him to another wedding where he did well beyond our wildest dreams. She believed he would be able to do so again.

Despite this previous success, I had some trepidation. I was concerned he would spoil the occasion by making loud vocalizations during the ceremony. Kara encouraged me to at least give him a chance.

The sunset over the cactus-lined mountain was spectacular. Friends and family were quiet as bride and groom affirmed their love and commitment to each other. Kyle was quiet too, somehow knowing. How could he know without really understanding? Or is that just an assumption we make? I can only wonder. How many other things do we make assumptions about, and go on to eliminate as options for Kyle?

Later, at the edge of the dance floor, Kyle danced and hummed to the powerful beat of the music. He was just another guest smiling and enjoying the moment. I watched with pride and deep appreciation as Kyle rose to this very special occasion. I am profoundly grateful he had the opportunity to participate.

Kara has been in Kyle's life for so long she has become part of our family. Kara is one of a handful of people who have inspired me to open doors of opportunity for Kyle. They are the believers. They have been open and willing to do whatever it takes to help him be the best he can be. Whether it involved going to school, traveling, or attending a wedding, they encouraged me to raise my expectations and believe more is always possible.

"Gayle and I had been doing our home-based programs for about ten years. One Saturday, during our phone conversation, we kidded each other about how, at age ninety, we'd still be calling each other and talking about what we'd done that week with our guys and our programs."

—Kathy

Taking Care

My Turn

Kathy

Being Mark's mom means that most of the time I'm busy taking care of him. Some days, I'm the one who needs care. There are days when just getting out of bed is more than I can handle. That's when it's time for the troops to come and rescue me. Yesterday was one of those days. The troop's name is Frank. He's also my husband.

He decided to take us on a Sunday drive. We piled into the car. Mark sat up front with Frank, keeping him company while Michael and I chilled in the back. Michael was asleep before we got out of the driveway. He had woken up really early to go fishing and was tired. Me, I settled in with my pillow and was ready for the ride.

Frank turned south on Highway 441. We've lived in this area for a very long time and have seen most of it, or so I thought. Frank started taking turns, just letting the spirit guide him, and the next thing I knew, we were traveling back roads, seeing stretches of country that were new to us. They were filled with pastures, farms, lakes, and little streams. We saw cypress trees and marshes—Florida in its lush summer prime. Soft mellow music on the radio provided the soundtrack for the outside moving movie.

We saw a restaurant by a lake and decided to stop. The restaurant owner greeted us. I asked her what kind of food she served, explaining that my son is sensitive to a lot of foods. She was open to fixing whatever he could eat. We stayed and had lunch, overlooking the lake, watching the alligators as they swam in front of us providing entertainment.

After dinner we headed home. One of my favorite memories as a child is the feeling I had at the end of a day's outing, sitting in the back seat of the car as my father drove us home. As the light of day changed into the darkness of night, I felt safe and secure. This is how I felt as we headed home.

Days like this are magical, fun, and inspiring. They renew my soul. A mini-vacation from my regular routine, I feel rested and replenished. Most of the time, I welcome the driver's seat, but yesterday it was nice to just sit back and leave the driving to him. I am grateful to Frank for the day.

Vacations

Gayle

Our family recently returned from our annual summer vacation. For many years, we have taken trips with our daughters, Rachel and Leah, leaving Kyle behind. We are fortunate to have exceptional help for Kyle so we can travel on a regular basis.

We always have enjoyed these summer holidays. They allow us to focus on enjoying our daughters, and give us a break from our somewhat rigorous family routine. The reality is, my husband Neil and I are often mentally, emotionally, and physically preoccupied with Kyle. Due to his special needs, he normally demands a lot from us and, at times, meeting his needs takes us away from giving as much attention to our daughters. While rising to the challenge of helping Kyle grow, I also have enjoyed and appreciated the ease with which my girls have grown and matured. It is a constant balancing act to meet the needs of all my children. I strive to take nothing for granted.

Our summer vacations are an incredible gift. In addition to the joy of traveling and seeing new places, we cherish the time we spend with our girls. We appreciate the ease with which we can all participate in activities, playing "typical family" for a week. Our parental responsibilities feel so light and easy during these times. We are again reminded of how special our daughters are to us. It has been great fun watching them experience new places and things, and they appreciate and enjoy the special attention they receive from us.

Vacations give me a much-needed break. At times, I feel worn out by the challenge of being Kyle's mom, and these trips recharge my body, mind and spirit. Though our trips are often full of activity, the changes in routine and reduced demands are rejuvenating.

For many years, I reasoned that Kyle probably wouldn't enjoy a vacation, since even routine changes were so difficult for him. I believed it would be more stressful than fun for Kyle, and therefore, also for the rest of the family. This was probably true during Kyle's younger years. He was so dependent on the familiar surroundings of his home that even going to the store, or to a friend's house, was an anxiety producing event.

These days, Kyle is better at handling changes in routine. Last summer, in addition to our family vacation, we took Kyle on a weekend trip to Sea World and the beach. Though it was definitely challenging for him, he did wonderfully during the entire adventure—staying in the hotel, eating out, waiting in lines. He even seemed to enjoy most of the experience. Of course, we did everything at a much slower pace, and focused specifically on his needs and what he might enjoy. Anticipating this, I had prepared to go with the flow. I had a wonderful time watching him soak up the new experiences and adapt in ways that probably weren't possible in years past. However, as enjoyable as this trip was, it was most definitely a working vacation.

Sometimes, I feel a twinge of guilt about excluding Kyle from our family vacations. In my heart, I believe everyone should be included. Realistically, it works best for Kyle to stay at home. I can truly rest and recharge, and offer my full attention to the rest of my family.

Life is a constant balancing act. Our vacations have become one of our family's keys to creating a healthy balance. Returning home refreshed and recharged, I am ready to take on what lies ahead with renewed energy and enthusiasm.

"We often end up laughing at our difficult moments, but not until they have passed."

—*Gayle*

Body and Soul

Walking

Kathy

I love to walk. The exercise is good, not only for my body, but for my mind and spirit as well. As I walk, I get to enjoy being outside, connecting to my world. I love to hear the birds sing accompanied by the distant sounds of the cars and trucks traveling down the highway—their backup chorus. I feel the cool breeze on my skin. The crickets trumpet the end of the day and announce the beginning of nightfall.

As I take this silent sojourn, I look up and see one lone bird sitting in a tree, looking down at me. I see my cows in the distance, grazing in the tall grass, and Mark sitting nearby, watching them. My husband, Frank, is watering his trees, while my older son, Michael, is driving the tractor in the field. Danie and Spring, my dog and cat, are walking with me.

I look up at the blue sky and white clouds, and my eyes fill with wonder and appreciation. It's a beautiful and peaceful time of the day. The sun is slowly setting, radiating its bright oranges, purples and reds. This live painting in front of me, with its entire majestic splendor, inspires me and I feel good.

I look back upon my day, and with each step, I let it go and come into this present moment. With head and heart clear, I am able to hear new ideas, new thoughts, and new insights that replenish and nurture me. I am renewed and ready for the opportunities and challenges that will come my way.

This is an important time for me. Mostly I walk because I love to, but it also helps me take better care of myself, and as a result, better care of my family. By filling my own well, body and soul, I am more useful, helpful and loving.

Filling My Well

Gayle

Step, shuffle, shuffle, ball change, ball change, ball change, CLAP! The steps echo in my mind. They are done at least twenty times faster than I can say them. I am hoping not to forget anything and smile and have style, all at the same time. If I happen to make a mistake, I just keep smiling and dancing.

These days I seem to have tap and jazz on the brain. Our big show is coming up and I've been having recital nightmares. What does dance have to do with raising a child with autism? Nothing, which is everything!

It's virtually impossible to dance without being in the present moment. That's what I love about it. When I go to class, my mind goes on vacation from all the concerns and thoughts I have about Kyle. I become carefree. For that time, I am just one of the other students in the class, and my biggest concerns are about keeping up and learning the steps. I am transported from the world of autism, meal preparation, and prompting, to the world of dance filled with shuffles, turns, and brush steps.

Dance class ends at 9:00 p.m. I come home and get the nightly report. "Kyle went swimming, and then was in and out of the refrigerator most of the evening seeking snacks," my husband, Neil, says. "He was very active, but in a good mood."

The words bounce off of me. I am still in the world of dance thinking about the roll-off. One, two, three, four, five, six, seven, eight—everything is in counts of eight. "Oh yes, and Kyle ate a whole jar of pickles." But, what was that step? The one we do before we take our bows? On Tuesday evenings, I am a free woman and pickles don't matter.

Dance is a wonderful challenge and diversion for me. I love where my mind goes when my body is in tap class. Dancing refills my well. For many years, I lived and breathed Kyle. I did this for so long, I didn't realize how dry my well had become. Dancing is one of the ways I found to replenish myself. Dancing, I am in the bless*ed* moment, and there's no place else to go.

"Gayle took me to their cabin in the mountains on my visit to Arizona. It's a beautiful place to rest, hike, and enjoy the scenic views. After a day of hiking and talking, we sat in the evening light, sharing more thoughts, dreams, and stories, as we warmed our bodies in front of the fire from the wood stove."

—Kathy

Attitude is Everything

What I'd Do Differently

Kathy

What would I do differently if I were starting my journey with Mark again? I would change my attitude. It would have been so useful and helpful to me if I could have embraced and loved this journey right from the start.

Having a child who is different presented me with both opportunities, and questions I had no idea how to answer. If I could have applied the concept of "so what" immediately, how much more fun the whole experience would have been. To laugh, accept, and greet all the new experiences and events that came to us—wow, what a gift. We would have been enveloped in grace, protected, and guided every step of the way. Enjoying our unique journey, we would have been free from the pressure to do things perfectly, trusting that there were no wrong moves—that it was all part of the process.

A couple weeks ago, I was sitting in a restaurant having breakfast with my parents and my sister. In a booth across the room sat a mom, dad, and their two children. They caught my attention by their noisiness in this otherwise quiet restaurant. They were too busy having a great time with each other to notice how noisy they were. The husband and wife sat across from each other, and she touched his foot underneath the table while they laughed and played with their children. Their happiness was infectious and inspiring.

I think of the times we as a family have been able to enjoy each other, free from all the seriousness that can surround us. It feels right to me.

So, if I could do it again, I would bring a lot more of that happiness into the picture—lots of laughter and a relaxed attitude, trusting that wherever we ended up was the right place for us. So, I practice this attitude today, knowing that it's a very good place to be.

What If?

Gayle

I am truly relieved Kyle is nineteen and past his childhood. I had so much angst and worry about the future when he was a little boy. Life was colored by my desperation to do the right thing. I could never do enough. Sick days or rest days were not allowed for either of us. The window of opportunity often seemed on the verge of closing, so I had to cram it all in before it slammed shut.

In reflection, what if my attitude was the only thing on this journey that mattered? What if I had known it was never too late? What if I had really believed that with all my heart? Would I have worried less? Felt less desperate to get the hours in, rushing from one thing to the next, cramming in as much stimulation as possible?

What if I had realized early on that everything I did with Kyle was really therapy anyway? What if, in the end, many of the things I was frantic and anxious about didn't really matter?

What if I could have previewed some of the lessons still to come in a crash course called acceptance? If I had believed there was plenty of time, would I have slowed down and really seen the unique soul of my child? Could I have looked past the labels to discover his extraordinary spirit? Could I simply love my boy for a while, without needing him to perform?

What if I had known he wasn't going to talk, would he be okay anyway? Could I then have been satisfied, even happy?

What if the number of hours, or even the type of therapy, didn't matter in the long run? Would I have allowed him to rest when he was sick? Could he have ditched a session once in awhile? Could I have spent a day holding him and seen that as productive?

What if Kyle's relationships with people mattered more than any other thing he achieved in his life? Would I have done it differently? Let him hug me to get out of working? Spend a session tickling and chasing, rather than matching and imitating?

We are now living the future I worried about for so long. There are no more age deadlines to meet. The developmental windows, if they ever really existed, have faded into the background. The doors of possibility are wide open, and we have plenty of time to explore them.

What if my attitude really *is* the only thing on this journey that matters?

"I love the way we brainstorm together on the phone. We both get great ideas for whatever we're working on at the time."

—*Gayle*

Making Room

Hope

Kathy

Sometimes I feel discouraged and overwhelmed. My spirit becomes tired and I want to find a place to lie down and cast off the demanding dynamics of my life. Instead, I find myself trying to operate as if everything around me *isn't* pulling at me, and go on as usual.

But sometimes, it's good just to stop and listen. Yesterday was one of those days. I felt particularly vulnerable and tired, spiritually and physically. I had received the monthly email from one of my favorite inspirational writers, Sark. She wrote that when you're feeling overwhelmed, it's time to stop and be present with what is going on, instead of trying to create something new.

So, I quit trying to go on as if I wasn't feeling what I was feeling. I sat on one of the rockers on our front porch and rocked. I listened to my heart, thoughts, and body. I felt myself "center." I no longer felt troubled by the fact that I felt overwhelmed and discouraged. I just sat with my feelings, and as I did, I felt better. And even though I still didn't have the answers, I felt rested and at peace.

When I got up, instead of trying to do anything differently, I stayed present. Mark, who had not slept for the past forty-eight hours, was in a demanding mood and needed me to fix something. Instead of trying to get him to let it go, I decided to be there with him and help him find and fix whatever "it" was.

I listened to my tiredness and gave myself an easy day. I took breaks, resting my body and spirit.

Slowly, my energy started to build and I felt renewed and ready to begin again. I was able to walk, and work in the garden. I was able to welcome my guys without flinching as they came near. I was able to enjoy the beauty around me, once more becoming aware of nature in all her splendor—the birds flying overhead, the tall field grass which now reached as high as the fence, and the magnificent sky dressed in multi-hued blues from the approaching evening storm. Hope filled my heart and lungs with fresh air, restoring the balance in my aching soul, and giving me the substance I needed. I smiled.

Letting Go

Gayle

It's been a little over two years now since Kyle began attending school full-time—about the same length of time we have been writing this book. Kyle's life is now very different from most of his childhood. He is comfortably settled in school, and participates in outside activities that don't directly involve me. While spending time away from each other during the day has been essential to Kyle's growth and development, and my own, letting go has been challenging, and sometimes even painful for me.

After eleven years of teaching Kyle at home, I was tired and worn out. Physically, I might have been able to go on forever. Mentally and emotionally, I was finished. My well had almost run dry. Initially, it was hard for me to acknowledge this, even to myself. I simply didn't know what else to do. I was "stuck" in doing my own home school program because of my fears and beliefs about the outside world. I was afraid of change and the unknown.

Then one day, one of Kyle's doctors asked me a pivotal question: "Why isn't Kyle in school?" Previously, I would have defensively said that being at home was the best way to meet Kyle's needs. Kyle's home program was my life, and prior to this, I was not open to doing things differently.

I suppose that question came at just the right time because I no longer had an answer to it. My previous reasons didn't make sense to me anymore. Thinking about it, though, I wanted to cry. Reexamining all the beliefs I had about stopping a home program would be an emotional journey. All of my fears about school, and outsiders working with Kyle, loomed large. So, when I finally did begin observing potential school programs, I found many I didn't like. I was almost glad to find this evidence so I could reconfirm to myself that no other options for Kyle existed.

I thought about the long term, and how someday Kyle and I would not be together. Reluctantly, I admitted to myself that it might be good for him to be with people who I had not trained extensively. Kyle needed to learn how to function in a world not orchestrated and controlled by me. I wanted to let go, for Kyle's sake and mine.

I looked deep into my heart to discover what it was I wanted for Kyle at this juncture in his life. I wanted him to broaden his horizons and become part of a more expansive world than I could provide for him at home. I dreamed of seeing him become more independent, and I wanted him to meet people similar to himself and develop new relationships.

What did I want for me? Was it okay to remove some of the self-imposed pressure to do it all for Kyle? I longed for more freedom and the ability to pursue other interests. I craved space to breathe, and think, and be. I wanted the opportunity to refill my well.

The process of finding a good school program for Kyle required lots of letting go, trust, and faith. I had to trust my instincts when things didn't seem right, and yet maintain my faith that I would eventually find something. I had to persist, and trust that others had good intentions for the young man I was so devoted to. I had to let go of needing to control.

So, Kyle went out into the world and learned to communicate with people who didn't know him well. He learned to bowl, enjoy field trips, and perform school jobs. He formed relationships with people I barely knew. He had never had these opportunities before.

These days, I continue to dance the dance of autism with my handsome young man. However, now my role is more mom than teacher or therapist. Easing up on some of the ties that bound me to Kyle has helped him broaden his horizons, learn, and mature. Yes, I still consider myself the best expert on Kyle, and regularly offer my expertise to the school staff, yet more and more, I am able to step back and observe without feeling the need to correct. Autism no longer colors every corner of my world. There is now more room for me. Slowly, the water level in my well is rising and that feels really, really good.

"One April, when Gayle came to visit me, I took her to one of my favorite places in the world, Crescent Beach. She and I sat on the beach in the cold windy spring air, and looked out at the ocean as we played writing games, asking each other journaling questions we made up as we went along. Little did we know then that one day we would write a book together."

—Kathy

Gentle Surrender

Grace

Kathy

Sometimes, when I reflect on my journey with Mark, I realize the thing that has always carried me through has been a state of grace.

Grace comes in silently during the night when I'm not looking, and stays with me throughout the day. Like an unseen hand on my shoulder, it's constantly there to guide, encourage, and protect me as I walk through uncharted territory. It's the silent voice that lets me know which way to go, what things to do, and when it's time to let go and do things differently. It's in the people who come and help me along the way when I'm feeling tired, discouraged, or ready to quit.

It's the same flowing energy that comes into my soul and moves through my body, filling me with new hope and renewed vigor to get into the game again. Like gentle hands that wrap around me and give me a sense of warmth and security when I'm feeling lost and doubting my every move, grace helps me know all is right with my world.

Grace is in each of the smiles and eyes of love I encounter, and most of all, in the face of my son, Mark, as he and I walk on this journey together. It is our shield, surrounding and protecting us. It guides us through each day, and points us in the right direction—toward our rainbow—making our way easy to follow.

Grace is my blessing and spiritual vitamin. I would be eternally lost without it. But, because it is there, the way is clear and I continue on, knowing that my final destination will be easy to find because of it.

Peace

Gayle

A friend of mine, who is the mother of a child newly diagnosed with autism, recently wrote to me: "At what point did you find peace? You seem so at ease with it all. I want to be there someday."

I was pleased to read someone saw that within me, and wondered about the answer. I wish I could go back and pinpoint the moment peace arrived, and know exactly how I got to that point. Though I would like to think it was one moment, I realize it was just a part of the process—a blurry point on my journey.

I was not always at peace. For a long time, especially during the early years, I was often in a state of angst. My heart ached most of the time. I was worried about the future, and concerned about whether or not we were using the right program and treatments. I was riddled with self-doubt, and no matter how much I did, it rarely felt like enough.

Early on, I had an intense desire to fix Kyle. From the moment I realized he was autistic, I entered into a fighting mode. I wanted to fix, repair, and eliminate the autism. I was prepared to do all I could to transform Kyle into "normal." Sometimes "normal" appeared deceivingly close.

As long as I was in fighting mode, inner peace eluded me. The thought, "my child wasn't supposed to be this way," was eating me up. To get out of this mode, I had to give up the struggle.

Because our thoughts help create our feelings, both the anxious and the blissful, I could struggle to make it go away—this thing that wasn't supposed to be, this enemy that stole my child—or I could relax, give up the fight, and create a shift in my perception. I had a choice. What if autism was *not* my enemy, but instead, my friend? What if "different" could become beautiful? What if, after acknowledging that Kyle wasn't supposed to be this way, I could let go and realize that God had different plans for our family? I began to discover it was my attitude and perspective that could either rob me, or give me, inner peace.

My friend is right. For the most part, I am at peace. Might it be the peace naturally felt by the parent of an older autistic child? Perhaps it is the peace that comes from truly acknowledging and accepting where Kyle is, and what he can do at this point in his life. Possibly, it's the peace that comes from allowing him time to enjoy his solitary, self-stimulating activities, without judgment. Just maybe, it's knowing what I want for him, but not needing those things to happen.

My desire is to dream unlimited dreams for Kyle and help him grow and learn as much as possible. I do this by making autism my friend instead of my enemy. I allow myself those unhappy moments, then dust myself off and begin again, moving forward on my journey, free to enjoy Kyle, autism and all.

"When I have felt overwhelmed, or just plain unhappy, wishing things were easier, Kathy has always been just a phone call or an email away. So many times during our conversations, we have quickly discovered we've had similar experiences with our sons, and with the way we have felt. This has always been a great comfort."

—*Gayle*

In The Moment

Happiness

Kathy

Last night, Frank saw the movie, "The Terminal." He loved the movie and said it was a great reminder for him that life is a process, not a destination. He said, "As in the example of Mark's seizures, instead of saying we'll be happy when they're gone, we'll be happy now." Happiness already lives within us. It is only our judgments and beliefs that tell us otherwise.

On a day-to-day basis, it's amazing how often I get to use this information. I look back at my own life and see how many times I have used happiness as my motivator. I'll be happy when I lose those extra five pounds, or when I get married and have children, or when we build our dream home. The list goes on and on. There was always something I could dangle in front of myself to motivate me to get what I wanted, with the prize of being happy.

Nothing is a better example of this than Mark. With his autism and seizures, I have been constantly motivated to help him. Behind that motivation was my desire for us to feel good and be happy. But what happens if you don't get what you want? Does that mean we must spend our whole lives being unhappy? Or must we be at the mercy of getting what we want so we can feel good?

I realized I didn't want to live my life this way anymore, dependent on things outside of me to be a certain way for me to feel good, whether that involved people or circumstances. I know now that happiness is the *way,* not the destination.

This has been an extraordinary gift. I love my life and the people in it. With its opportunities and challenges, each day is like a brand new canvas on which I get to paint. Some days I love what I create, and other days, not so much. As I practice my skills in the art of living, I am getting much better at it. And just like painting, my "pictures" might not be perfect, but I'm having fun, living and "painting" my life.

Hungry

Gayle

After twenty years, I still have an insatiable appetite for information. I am still hungry to learn the latest about autism. I crave a better understanding of my son, Kyle. I want answers. With each new piece of information, I add a few more pieces to the puzzle that is autism, and the enigma that is Kyle.

Supposedly, knowledge is power. However, despite the wealth of available information, there are many times when I feel more powerless than powerful, more confused than clear, and more uncertain than confident. What is it I seek? A better understanding of my silent son.

God forgot to include the instruction manual when he sent Kyle, and I am still waiting for it to be written. The questions echo in my mind. On a moment-to-moment basis, what information is most useful? What guidelines will point me in the right direction? What words will inspire me to stay passionate and motivated on this journey, rather than throw my hands up in frustration or resignation? A guidebook would be nice. Do this, this, and this, it would say. I would like to have that book on my bedside table.

However, what I really hunger for is what speaks to my heart. Deep down, I realize what matters most is who I am when I sit with Kyle and wait for him to respond to something I have asked a hundred times before.

My soul yearns for something that will touch my spirit and maintain my courage, words that will boost my strength and offer support. Then,

I will have the emotional vigor to continue greeting another day of routines with Kyle. Then, I can continue to see the possibilities for growth.

Without this instruction manual, it is up to me to make choices that will help Kyle be the best he can be. Trial and error prevails. Hope and perseverance reign. What I have learned is, as I learn to see him differently, and help him in different ways, I see myself and life differently as well.

Each evening, in the moment I look into Kyle's eyes and he returns my gaze, my life feels complete. Researchers might speculate that his cerebral cortex has scrambled neurons. He might have trouble putting on his socks. It doesn't matter. We are making a familiar connection with each other once again. In that moment, my appetite is satisfied.

"People have asked what I consciously did to evolve emotionally over the years. Writing has been one of my growth and change instruments. Kathy inspired me to begin writing. It took her awhile to convince me to pick up the pen. Sometimes we would just make lists of things we were grateful for."

—*Gayle*

Trust Life

Life is Good

Someone once asked me, "What would have helped you back then?" What could I have read or heard in the beginning that would have helped me on this journey with my special son? My answer was, "I would have wanted someone to tell me it would all be okay."

This someone would have told me I didn't have to worry, because in the end, everything would work out. For every question I had, there would be an answer, and my path, although not always easy, would be one I could follow. I would find the way to help Mark be healthy and experience a sense of well being. There were no time limits. We would get there when we got there.

This someone would have told me not to worry about making mistakes, because they are all part of the process of developing our skill as travelers. I was starting a journey, and while at first I might feel frightened by the unknown, I would have everything I need within me to carry me through. I would discover new strength and courage I never knew I had, and with each step, I would become more of the person I was meant to be, beyond anything I could ever have imagined.

This someone would have told me I would learn to trust myself, growing stronger and more confident as I came to rely on that voice inside of me, even when it differed with the professionals and books. I would know that as his parent and champion, I knew Mark better than anyone else, and I could count on my instincts, even in the face of disagreement or disapproval. What an amazing gift this would turn out to be.

I would know to believe and trust in my dreams—that they are inspired by God. Believing in my dreams opens windows and doorways to endless possibilities, bringing me that much closer to my vision.

With all this to guide me, I would come to believe and trust in myself and not fear anything on this journey, because even should I falter and fall, I would always have the "hand" reaching down and helping me get up and begin again.

It *is* all okay, because I know, in my heart of hearts, I can trust life, and life is good. We were sent here for a reason. We belong.

Knowing this back then would have helped me. It is what I know now. Trust life. It is good, so very good.

A Vision for the Future
Gayle

One day, as I was walking along peacefully, Kyle's adulthood crept up and tapped me on the shoulder. I knew it was coming, and yet it caught me off guard, because when I look at photos of Kyle as a little boy, it seems like just yesterday, yet also feels like another lifetime.

Kyle has two years of high school left. Technically and emotionally, it was an ordeal to get him into school in the first place, at the age of sixteen. I really haven't wanted to think about what would happen when he became too old to go. I have been enjoying the lull before the next big decision-making process begins.

So what does my heart desire for Kyle after school is over? My dream for him is what most parents want for all their children—happiness. I wish him to have happy, fulfilling days as he continues to mature and grow. But, how do I know what fulfillment is to Kyle when he offers few clues? This is my dilemma. I must plan his life around my desires for him, while trying not to allow any of my limiting beliefs to place too many restrictions on him.

I yearn for Kyle to continue his education after school ends, and throughout his life. While he will still receive education at home, can I find a day program that will continue to teach rather than merely babysit? My vision for him includes physical exercise and community participation. Is there a job Kyle could do that he would not find aversive? I don't want to torture him for the sake of fulfilling my idea of a meaningful life.

Carrying this faint sketch of a vision, I already have ventured out to glance at what day programs might be available. Fortunately, I've teamed up with other moms so I would not be doing this alone. I've seen many programs I knew were not where I would want Kyle to spend his days. It is likely we will need to create our own program. Once again, my heart aches at the thought of the unknown.

Since two years will pass quickly, I must explore the possibilities. However, part of me does not want to see or explore. I prefer to stay right here and freeze time. I'm not quite ready to cut any new trails up the mountain. Will I be ready when the time comes? Will Kyle?

If I am to be prepared, I must reluctantly continue to crawl out of my cave and take a peek around. As on all other legs of this journey, there is no guidebook specifying a particular path or giving definitive answers. There are only possibilities based on what has already been done, or what I choose to create. I will make mistakes, and then correct my course. As always, it comes back to trusting my own instincts—that I will arrive at the right place eventually.

With optimism and uncertainty, I welcome the arrival of Kyle's adulthood. Looking toward the future, I wait with anticipation as the next set of doors open ahead of me. I have confidence in myself to discover the path that will get us there, wherever "there" might be.

"*Gayle and I love to shop. We've only met about five times since (we have more of a phone relationship), but each time we do, the number one thing on our agenda is to go shopping. Once, in a mall in Orlando, Fla., we found a bathing suit store. An hour later, after trying on every single style of bathing suit there, we came out of our perspective dressings rooms, laughing and exhausted, filled with joy. Did we ever buy one? I don't remember.*"

—*Kathy*

Hope Springs Eternal

My Dream

Kathy

I have a dream that one day Mark will no longer have autism or a seizure disorder. He will emerge into this world as a young man, free from the maladies that once held him.

I have had this dream since he was a little boy. During the years we worked with Mark on the Son Rise program, this dream was the fuel that motivated each hour of each day. Every waking moment, I prayed and hoped for this dream to become a reality. And, although my dream is still a dream, I believe in it now as strongly as I did then.

I love my son just as he is right now, autism, seizures and all. But, I still want more for him. I want him to be free to talk and express who he is without struggling for the words. I want him to be able to sleep through the night seizure free, and wake up with the knowledge his day will be the same. I want his food sensitivities to be a thing of the past, freeing him to eat without worrying about getting sick. I want each day to be like a banquet filled with opportunities from which he is free to choose. And, while his life is filled with love and friends, I want even more for him.

This dream is in me, and while there have been many times I have wanted to throw it away or give up on it, it always comes back. It is alive and well in my heart, sometimes occasionally showing its face, and other times walking silently beside me, holding my hand.

In her book, *The Artist's Way,* Julia Cameron writes, "My dreams come from God, and God has the power to accomplish them." I hold this thought close to me as I take each step toward making my dream a reality. I find ways to help me focus and stay on course.

Sometimes, it's hard for me to think this dream can come true because it hasn't yet. Then I remember one of my favorite movies, "A Knight's Tale," and I believe again.

The story takes place in medieval times and tells of a young man whose dream is to become a knight. Because of his "class," this is not permitted, ever. One had to be of royal birth to become a knight. While a young boy, he is told fulfilling his dream is akin to changing the stars in the sky—impossible. He asks his father if this is true. His father responds, "William, anything is possible, if only you believe." William goes on, never giving up on his dream, and becomes the very thing everyone around him thought impossible.

This movie inspires me to hold on to my dream. I, too, believe. I believe it is possible for my son to emerge from autism, even when most would say it is not. In the meantime, I'll keep going, loving my son as he is and believing in all he can be. And so it is, and so it will be.

The Cure

Gayle

Last week, I touched on emotions I haven't experienced in a long time. The last time I felt these emotions, I was at an autism fundraiser. While there, I wrote, "There must be a piece of my heart that still grieves for the Kyle that never was." Kathy, posing as perceptive detective, said, "Maybe the grieving you say you feel for Kyle isn't grieving at all, but a longing for the things you want, but are afraid to want, because you don't think they're possible." This was great food for thought. Was my old dream of a cure still lurking below the surface?

The cure was the carrot I dangled in front of myself during the early years of doing my home program. I always came back to the question, could I be happy if Kyle remained autistic? I wanted the answer to be yes, but found it difficult. I celebrated his progress, and yet I often held back because no matter what special thing he accomplished, he was still autistic.

I spent years chasing the carrot, needing and wanting Kyle to somehow emerge from autism. Fueled by passion and enthusiasm, and also desperation and dissatisfaction, I drove myself hard. Reflecting back, I wonder if this kept me from fully appreciating Kyle and enjoying more of my time with him. Had Kyle been getting the message I was never quite satisfied with him?

Several years ago, I began to shift in my thinking. Kyle was getting older, and his differences were becoming more pronounced. In addition to his autism, he faced many other challenges and had not made as much progress as I had hoped. I began to view autism more as a way of being, than a disorder or illness. The more I was able to do this, the lighter I began to feel. My need to change the outcome began to diminish.

I learned a lot from the first part of my journey, when my dream and focus were on a cure. Perhaps, it was all to prepare me for the second part. My passion and enthusiasm remain as I have evolved from wanting to fix the autism, to wanting to provide as many opportunities as possible for Kyle's growth and independence, despite his autism.

I suppose there is always the ultimate "what if" question. If a pill or treatment were discovered that would cure Kyle's autism, would I go for it? Though not something I think about very often anymore, I occasionally wonder what Kyle might have been like without autism and the other difficulties he faces. If he were able to communicate with words, would we know Kyle better, and he us? Certainly, life would have been different, but perhaps this is like wondering what life would have been like with another husband, or if my daughters had been boys.

Autism is entwined within Kyle's essence. It is a way of being that sometimes gets in his way, and mine. It is also part of what makes him the unique, lovable soul he is. I strive to view autism as a gift, as well as a challenge.

Kyle has blossomed, and I expect he will continue to do so. It feels good to know that my heart's desire for him, that he be the best Kyle he can be, has evolved over the years. I am on a path that brings me comfort and allows me the most freedom and acceptance.

So, am I still afraid to want? Deep down, do I still crave that cure? I don't have an answer. My focus is very much on enhancing the quality of Kyle's life without a specific end result or dream in mind. Certainly, at times, I wish things were easier for both of us, however I'm not convinced a cure would be the answer.

There is a saying, "Be careful what you wish for. You might just get it." Maybe someday, before a child with autism is born, science will be able to alter his brain and prevent it. Is this a good thing? I'm not so sure. Perhaps not needing the cure *is* the cure.

"Kathy has been my support, my sounding board, my shoulder to cry on, my rock, my nonjudgmental questioner, my mirror to learn the strongest and weakest in me, my guide to seeing things in a light-hearted way, the instigator of many good laughs, my creative inspiration, my companion, and my long-distance soul sister on this journey of living."

—*Gayle*

The Truth Will Set You Free

The Gardening of Life

Kathy

Yesterday, after I finished writing, I decided to work in the garden. I went to the barn, picked up the hoe, and headed out to my garden to start digging. The potato plants had already been harvested, so my goal was to clean up the first row, which was full of weeds. I soon discovered lots of potatoes that still needed pulling, so I dug in.

Shortly into my work, with beads of perspiration pouring off my skin, I realized I needed to fortify myself for the work ahead. I put the hoe down and went into the house to get my hat, put on sunscreen and my bathing suit-shorts combo, and grab a huge bottle of water. Now ready, the heat of the steamy day climbing, I joined nature and began my job of working the land. I had fun.

Today, my shoulders and neck are sore, but I have a basket full of potatoes, and my row in the garden is ready for the next crop. I realize that, as I had worked, I listened to the earth. The air, although hot and humid, teamed rich with life, just beckoning me to create and fulfill some ancient destiny. I felt it. I had worked the land, sweat flowing off of me, drinking lots of water. I felt connected and a part of the world. I know I am a living part of this season. I feel good.

My dreams for Mark are similar to planting a garden. I plant the seeds of my desires and carefully work my dreams. I create a loving and safe environment where he is able to flourish and grow. I pull out the weeds—the areas of resistance, and beliefs that threaten to choke any new growth—giving him room to grow. I work it daily, paying careful

attention to the continually evolving process. We're building new path-
ways, and like the vegetables springing from the earth, we are both
transforming.

I find myself falling in love with the process and am rewarded with
the fruit of my labors, as I see both of us growing and becoming all we
can be.

Life is good.

Is Autism Something You Have or Something You Are?

Gayle

Kathy and I have been discussing this for a while. Do our sons have autism or are they autistic? What's the difference? If I see autism as something Kyle has, similar to an illness, then it might imply it could go away some day. If I see autism as a way of being, it implies it is permanent.

For a long time, I prayed, hoped, and worked for a cure for Kyle's autism because I saw it as bad for him, and bad for me. I did not want a label to define who he was. I believed we were both cheated—Kyle, because he would not be able to experience life as a "normal" person, and me, because I would not be able to have a relationship with a "normal" son.

During the last few years, I have been influenced by Jim Sinclair, an autistic man who wrote a speech entitled, "Don't Mourn for Us." Sinclair says it is not possible to separate the autism from the person, as he believes autism is pervasive, coloring every experience, sensation, perception, thought, emotion, and encounter. In other words, it colors every aspect of existence. Contemplating a cure, he says, "If it were possible, the person you'd have left would not be the same person you started with." I suspect I had been thinking this way for a while, but had been reluctant to admit it, fearing that it meant I was giving up on Kyle becoming "normal."

Thinking of autism in this way has had a profound impact on me. I tried to imagine what it would be like to live in a world where people wished you were a different person much of the time. Is this what I was doing by wishing for a cure? Did Kyle need to be fixed, or did I?

When I believed Kyle's autism could be cured, I sometimes looked at him and saw "not enough." In many ways, I was holding out for "someday." Someday we will get rid of autism, find the boy inside, and set him free. Then, I too would be free. I shared society's prejudice against children who are born and labeled "different." I wanted my life to be easier, something I saw as possible only if Kyle was "normal."

I understand Kyle in a different way now, a way that allows me to accept him on a deeper level than before. I now see autism as very much a part of who he is. I recognize, more than ever, the challenges he faces by perceiving the world so differently.

We do our best to understand each other. At times, I struggle as much as he does. I must overcome my own handicaps and limiting beliefs to form connections with him. I find new dimensions in myself in the process. Kyle takes me to uncomfortable and uncertain places and essentially says, "Here, deal with this." By asking him to work hard to overcome his challenges and make connections, I, in turn, also must work hard to do the same.

If I see autism as all encompassing, does that mean I am defining Kyle with a label? And, if so, does that limit his possibilities? I've discovered that, to the contrary, seeing autism this way has set me free, and hopefully, has done the same for Kyle. My new level of acceptance has lightened my emotional load, and I have opened up to seeing and providing new opportunities and experiences for Kyle. The possibilities are endless.

"Gayle and I are like the different seasons in which we were born. She's a winter and I'm a summer. She drinks tea and I like coffee. She hikes in the mountains and I take long walks on the beach. She lives in the city and I live in the country. She lives in the Southwest and I live in the Southeast. She loves ice cream and I love cake. We're different, but like soup and a sandwich, our friendship goes so well together."

—Kathy

Mark

Thanksgiving

Kathy

*Mark is my Teacher. **T**aking my hand, we walk together.*
*I learn that **H**appiness is our guide and map,*
not our destination.
The two of us are on an
***A**dventure that leads to valleys of beauty and wonder,*
mountains of amazing challenges, seas of wide-open mystery . . .
ever playful and sometimes fearful, we walk.
He shows me how to dance along the way and I learn to let go of my
***N**eed to control.*
***K**eeping the faith, we journey on, even when all the*
evidence points elsewhere, trusting all is well.
*He shows me how to **S**ee in a new way and*
I watch as the pre-existing
boundaries crumble, opening to a broader and more expansive view.
*Each day I **G**row, becoming stronger and more comfortable in*
my own skin, under his wise and careful tutoring.
***I** am*
***V**ictorious*
With each mountain we climb, facing and mastering
the challenges and obstacles in front of us.
*And **I**,*
*i**N***
*Trusting and **G**iving my heart and hand*
To this special soul, learn to see the beauty in everything.